Cards
galore

D1557912

Fransie Snyman

Cards
galore

STACKPOLE
BOOKS

Published by Stackpole Books
5067 Ritter Road
Mechanicsburg, PA 17055
www.stackpolebooks.com

First published in 2012
by Metz Press
1 Cameronians Avenue
Welgemoed, 7530
South Africa

Publisher	Wilsia Metz
Photographer	Ivan Naudé, Kenneth Irvine
Design and layout	Liezl Maree
Cover design	Wendy A. Reynolds
Translator	Amanda Taljaard
Proofreader	Christine de Nobrega
Reproduction	Robert Wong, Color/Fuzion
Print production	Andrew de Kock

Printed and bound in Singapore by Tien Wah Press

ISBN 978 0 8117 1267 5

Author's acknowledgements

Once again, a big thank you to my family
for your patience while I wrote the book,
and for taking the chaos at home in
your stride.

Thank you Corlé and Lynette who made
some of the cards.

Ansia – thank you so much for your
wonderful ideas and help with the edible
cards. You are incredibly talented and
display such amazing patience in the
creative process.

Thank you Ivan and Kenneth for the
lovely photographs and your relaxed
and knowledgeable approach during the
photo shoots.

Wilsia, thank you for another opportunity
to do a book. The going got tough at
times, but your calm and professional
direction always ensure the best possible
end product.

Liezl – thank you for your creative input
and making everything look great!

Above all else I thank our Heavenly
Father for giving me strength to
complete the project.

Contents

Introduction

In this electronic day and age, it is probably the easiest thing in the world to send someone an electronic card on a special occasion. It seems to be a trend these days simply to leave a message on one of the social network pages to wish someone a happy birthday or to celebrate a special event.

However, there are few things worth more than a handmade card. Making cards has a dual purpose – it is very therapeutic for the creator, and it brings joy to the receiver. The greatest gift you can give someone is time – your time. When you make a card with loving care for a specific person, you definitely give a little of yourself.

Handmade cards are usually beautiful enough to be displayed, or even framed. And you would be surprised to see how quickly one can make a card – it is much faster than shopping for one!

The purpose of this book is mainly to explain basic techniques and to provide ideas for making your own cards. The techniques are explained step by step so that even someone who has never made a card would also understand how to go about it. Whether you are a beginner or an experienced card maker, you will find something useful in this book.

The styles and techniques of card making are constantly changing, and I really like simple cards. If you prefer fine details, you are welcome to embellish and add a personal touch.

One can use anything to make cards – not only paper or card. The book even contains edible cards that can be made in a jiffy.

You will notice that I have used few words. That was done to enable you to choose your own wording for each card. Monica de Beer's book *Words for paper, art & craft creations*, ISBN 978 1 920268 58 9, published by Metz Press, is an excellent source of ideas for specific words and messages.

Materials and supplies

There are certain materials without which crafters, and especially card makers, cannot function. A list of the supplies for each project is provided. Make sure that everything is ready before you start to prevent a frustrating search once you are halfway. This section provides the basic requirements for the completion of most of the projects.

Basic materials

Cutting implements and mat

A good craft knife, scissors and guillotine are the most important tools for card making. You obviously also need a good cutting mat on which to work. The self-healing kind is the best choice. These can be used for years without showing signs of wear.

When you are using a ruler to measure what you are cutting, it is important to use a steel one. Plastic rulers are easily damaged by if you accidentally cut or nick them. I have also used deckle-edged scissors to cut fancy edges, and an oval cutter that comes with templates and blades.

When you are working with felt or material, use a pair of good fabric scissors. There are few things as frustrating as trying to cut felt with a pair of blunt scissors.

Glue and other adhesives

If you use the wrong glue for your card project, you can ruin the appearance of the card completely. Most crafters use specific, old favourites. I have used the following:

A glue pen – for very delicate pasting.

Double-sided tape – to stick ribbon to card, as well as to join large pieces of paper and card. It is available in various widths. I prefer to use the narrowest tape. If one accidentally pastes it askew, it can be removed more easily than a broader strip. To attach larger areas, I simply use more than one strip.

Glue wheel – to stick smaller pieces of paper and card together. It can be used instead of double-sided tape, but it is not as adhesive.

Glue dots – to fix trimmings to cards. The glue dots are available in various sizes and stick firmly to most surfaces.

Adhesive foam or foam squares – to add dimension to your cards. When you use it, the pasted object is slightly elevated, which adds dimension to the card.

Masking tape – to attach certain parts temporarily, for example for iris folding and when you are doing embossing work on a light box.

Craft punches

The variety of craft punches available today is amazing – I have a cupboard full and I would love to have more! The beauty of using punches is that one can create truly wonderful cards with little effort and paper. I am sure many card makers share this view. Even when using basic shapes such as squares, circles and hearts, you can create interesting pictures. In the chapter on punch work, I will describe the technique more thoroughly.

For the best results, you must look after your punches and always store them neatly. Manufacturers suggest different ways of sharpening punches. Some suggest that you punch through various layers of wax paper, while others say that you should punch through a few layers of aluminium foil. You should experiment to find what works for you. However, if you do not regularly use the punch on thick paper, it should remain sharp for some time.

Materials for stamping

Some of the projects in this book involve stamping. Stamping was especially popular when handmade cards came back into fashion. The stamps that were available then were mainly rubber ones mounted on wood. These are still popular and a large variety is available. Transparent stamps mounted on acrylic blocks are easier to use, because you can see exactly where your design will appear.

The inkpads and stamps obviously go together, and you will also find a variety of inkpads available nowadays. The projects in this book are embossed by using embossing powder on the stamps.

Stencils and embossing

A superb variety of stencils is available for embossing work. If it contains intricate details, the stencil is usually made of metal, but plastic ones are also readily available. You can even make your own stencil by cutting a pattern from thin, sturdy card.

Ink and glass paint

Alcohol ink is used to create the most exquisite backgrounds on glossy paper and non-porous surfaces. A special applicator is used to apply the paint to the background. Glass paint does not necessarily have to be used only on glass. It also works well on acetate and thick, transparent plastic.

Paper and cardstock

Paper and cardstock are available in various sizes and thicknesses. The mass of the paper is an indication of its thickness. Paper of 80 g/m² (grams per square metre) is suitable for everyday use and printing. Tissue paper can weigh as little as 15 g/m² and paper that is suitable for the making of cards varies between 160 g/m² and 250 g/m². I prefer working with paper that weighs 230 g/m² because it is not too thick and it folds easily. Paper that is thicker than 250 g/m² is regarded as cardboard. When I refer to cardstock in the material list, it includes any paper from 160–250 g/m².

Shops that stock scrapbook paper are inexhaustible sources of decorative paper. Because of the variety available today, you will hardly need anything more for your card making. Ordinary patterned paper is also readily available at craft shops and any shop that stocks paper.

Handmade paper is also extremely popular among card makers; even a dash of handmade paper can make a card look stunning.

Paper is available in various sizes, such as
A1 (594 mm × 841 mm),
A2 (420 mm × 594 mm),
A3 (420 mm × 297 mm) and
A4 (297 mm × 210 mm).

I have also made extensive use of scrapbook paper, which usually measures 12 × 12 inches (approximately 30,5 cm × 30,5 cm).

Embellishments

An assortment of embellishments is available to use on cards. Metal embellishments (charms), paper flowers, ribbons, handmade stickers, beads, split pens, buttons and glitter can be used to add the finishing touches to your work.

Other necessary tools

- **Bone folder** – to make indents and perfect folds in paper. It can also be used to flatten paper in order to ensure adhesion of layers.
- **Embossing pen** – a blunt-nosed tool, the points of which are two different sizes, used for embossing paper and metal.
- **Heat-gun** – used to emboss cards when embossing powder is used. It can also be used for general heating and melting.
- **Light-box** – to trace patterns, and when embossing is done using a template.
- **Teflon craft mat** – is available with a Teflon coating and can simplify your life. This specific mat protects your work surface against stains, glue and heat – nothing sticks to the mat.

Terminology and techniques

Some of the terminology and techniques that are applicable to most cards are explained here.

Cut, score and fold

It is far easier to buy pre-cut cards, but then you are restricted to what is available in shops. I usually buy larger pieces of cardstock and paper and cut it to the required sizes myself. Poor and skew cutting can really stand out and if you notice that something has not been cut neatly, you know others would notice it too. Make absolutely sure that the knife, scissors and guillotine that you are using are razor sharp to ensure straight, clean edges.

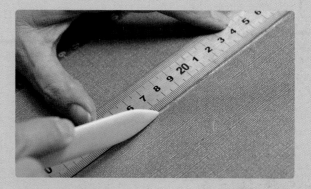

When you have finished cutting the cardstock, you can score it using a bone folder. It is easy to mark the fold line when working on a mat on which measurements are indicated. If your mat does not contain measurements, you can mark the fold line lightly in pencil. Mark the line using the bone folder, then fold along the line and flatten by pressing the bone folder on the fold and running it smoothly along its length.

Embossing

Motifs that are stamped on cards appear more beautifully finished if you sprinkle embossing powder over them and then heat them to melt the powder. Press the stamp on the cardstock and sprinkle embossing powder over the print. Heat carefully, using a heat-gun to melt the powder.

Ensure that the ink is still wet when you sprinkle the powder over it and be careful not to burn the paper.

Using templates and motifs

To make some of the cards in this book, you will have to copy a given template. The easiest way to do this would be to photocopy it or scan the image onto your computer. You can also use tracing paper. Should the templates need enlarging, it will be indicated clearly.

To attach ribbon to cardstock

It is sometimes difficult to prevent the glue from showing through or spreading around the ribbon when you are sticking ribbon to cardstock. This can ruin the card. The best way to attach ribbon to cardstock is to use the narrowest double-sided tape. This allows you to easily remove the ribbon if it is a little skew. It is easier to fix the double-sided tape to the paper first and then paste the ribbon onto it.

Matting

When you are pasting cardstock or paper of various sizes on top of one another, it is known as matting. Matting adds dimension to your work and can be used to emphasise certain aspects. Cut the consecutive layers so that each one differs by approximately 5 mm from the previous one.

Temporary adhesive

It is sometimes necessary to attach a template temporarily. The best way to do this is by using masking tape. Ordinary sticky tape can damage your cardstock.

Versatile folding techniques

If you fold a card in interesting ways, you need fewer embellishments. Using various folding techniques also cuts down on the equipment that you need. You simply need cardstock, paper, a ruler and a pair of scissors to produce extraordinary results. You can use any paper and the colours of your choice to create a truly unique product.

Gate fold

This is a very simple technique and the appearance of the card will be determined by the embellishments that you choose.

YOU WILL NEED

» Pink cardstock: 28 cm x 20 cm
» 2 pieces of patterned paper in shades that match the card-stock: 6,5 cm x 19,5 cm each
» 2 pieces of patterned paper that also match these colours: 5,5 cm x 18,5 cm
» Pink organza ribbon: 50 cm long and 1 cm wide
» Double-sided tape
» Glue wheel
» Ruler
» Bone folder

Method

1. Mark and score the pink card at 7 cm and 21 cm.
2. Fold the sides inward along the scored lines.
3. Apply glue to the larger pieces of patterned paper and paste these on the folded parts.
4. Repeat this step using the smaller pieces of patterned paper.
5. Apply double-sided tape to the reverse side, in the middle of the card. The tape must extend approximately 1,5 cm past the card – it is folded towards the front.
6. Peel off the backing tape.
7. Secure the ribbon and fold it over the front of the card.
8. Close the card and make a bow.

Gate fold variation

This is also a very simple technique and the type of paper that you choose will determine the appearance of the card. With the selection of beautiful paper that is available, you will be able to make this card quickly and easily.

YOU WILL NEED

» Brown cardstock:
  26 cm x 14 cm
» 1 piece of patterned paper
  in a shade that matches the
  cardstock: 13,3 cm x 11 cm
» 2 pieces of patterned paper
  that also match the rest:
  13,5 cm x 5,5 cm
» Glue wheel
» Border craft punch
» Ruler
» Bone folder

Method

1. Score the brown cardstock at 1 cm, 7 cm, 19 cm and 25 cm.
2. Fold the cardstock towards the inside along the 7 cm and
   19 cm scored lines, and then fold it back out along the 1 cm
   and 25 cm scored lines.
3. Punch the narrow-folded edges using the border punch.
4. Stick the smaller pieces of patterned paper on the inside and
   the larger piece on the outside.
5. If it looks as if the card is going to pop open, you can tie a
   ribbon around it.

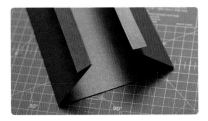

Z-fold

This card apparently derived its name from the way in which it is folded. It just goes to show that by using a simple fold, you can create a card that differs completely from conventionally folded ones. Patterned paper, strengthened at the centre with pink cardstock, is the base of this card.

YOU WILL NEED

» Patterned paper: 30 cm x 14 cm
» Pink pearlescent cardstock:
   10 cm x 11 cm
» 3 rhinestones
» Glue wheel
» Glue dots
» Border craft punch
» Ruler
» Bone folder

Method

1. Turn the patterned paper over so that you are looking at the reverse side.
2. Place the paper along its length from left to right.
3. Mark the paper at 14 cm on the right-hand edge, and at 7,5 cm on the left-hand edge. Connect the two points and cut along the line that you have drawn.

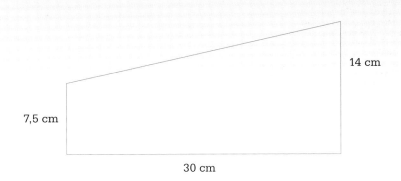

14 cm

7,5 cm

30 cm

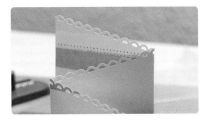

4. Score the paper at 9 cm and 19 cm.
5. Fold the left-hand side towards the inside and the right-hand side towards the outside along the scored lines.
6. The three panels that have been formed are now 9 cm, 10 cm and 11 cm wide respectively.
7. Paste the pink cardstock on the centre panel and cut at an angle along the edge of the panel.
8. Punch along the entire edge using the border punch.
9. The folded card should resemble the photo on the left.
10. Lastly, stick the three rhinestones in the centre of the front panel using the glue dots.

Two-in-one fold

I call this the two-in-one fold, because one actually makes two separate cards which are then interlinked and pasted together. It is also a very simple fold and the paper that you choose will determine the appearance of the card.

YOU WILL NEED

» Blue cardstock: 19 cm x 14 cm
» Brown cardstock (I used cardstock that is brown on one side and light yellow on the reverse side): 18 cm x 12 cm
» 1 piece of patterned paper: 6,5 cm x 13,5 cm
» 1 piece of patterned paper: 8,5 cm x 11,5 cm
» Glue wheel ruler
» Bone folder

Method

1. Score the blue cardstock at 13 cm and fold it towards the inside along the scored line.
2. Paste the patterned paper on the opposite side of the fold.
3. Score and fold the brown cardstock in half along the scored line.
4. Paste the patterned paper that matches the size onto it.
5. Stick the brown cardstock onto the blue cardstock, leaving the folds to close in opposite directions.
6. Be sure to position the brown cardstock exactly in the centre of the blue cardstock.

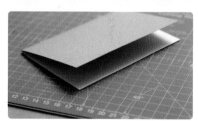

Easel cards

This card is flat but when you open it, it resembles an easel. It makes a beautiful display.

YOU WILL NEED

» Sturdy brown cardstock:
11 cm x 21 cm
» Sturdy brown cardstock
square: 11 cm x 11 cm
» Sturdy brown cardstock:
11 cm x 2,5 cm
» 2 pieces of matching
patterned paper:
10,5 cm x 10,5 cm each
» Extra patterned paper to
punch the flower
» 3–5 paper flowers
» Pink button
» Double-sided tape
» Glue wheel
» Glue dots
» Flower craft punch
» Ruler
» Bone folder

Method

1. Score the larger piece of brown cardstock at 11 cm and 16 cm.
2. Fold towards the inside along the 11 cm scored line and towards the outside along the 16 cm mark.
3. Decorate the brown cardstock square with the patterned paper, paper flowers and button. I used a punched paper flower of the same patterned paper under the paper flowers.
4. Place double-sided tape on the pieces of brown cardstock that were folded towards the outside.
5. Stick the decorated cardstock square onto the fold.
6. Use patterned paper to decorate the inside of the card.
7. Paste patterned paper on the small piece of brown cardstock and stick it to the base of the card. This ensures that the card will remain upright when you open it.

Crossover fold

This card cannot open once you have made it. It is actually an envelope or little bag for the card. You can change it to a card that can be unfolded if you remember not to glue the bottom flaps. You must bear in mind that the message will be visible when the card is folded.

YOU WILL NEED

- » Red cardstock: 30 cm x 15 cm
- » 2 pieces of red patterned paper: 9,5 cm x 14 cm each
- » White pearlescent cardstock for the heart
- » Patterned paper for the heart
- » Red ribbon: 20 cm long and 1 cm wide
- » Glue wheel
- » Double-sided tape
- » Ruler
- » Bone folder
- » Guillotine

Method

1. Score the red cardstock at 10 cm and 20 cm.
2. Fold the sides towards the inside along the scored lines. The outer panels are lying on top of each other.
3. Open the card and cut the side panels to curve from top to bottom.
4. Cut the patterned paper in the same way and paste it on the red cardstock.
5. Turn in the side panels and place a strip of double-sided tape along the base between the panels to seal the base flap completely.
6. Use the outline of the template on p. 192 and cut a heart from the patterned paper. Also cut a smaller heart from the white cardstock.
7. Paste the white heart on the patterned paper one.
8. Make a hole in the top of the heart through which red ribbon is threaded and tied.

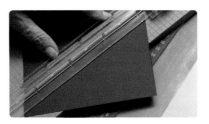 

Shell fold

This fold is very popular because it serves as a card and an envelope in one. It is ideally suited as a wedding invitation.

YOU WILL NEED

- » White textured paper: 21 cm x 21 cm
- » White pearlescent paper: 10 cm x 10 cm
- » 3 white paper flowers: different sizes
- » Silver-grey paste pearl
- » Silver pen
- » Glue dot
- » Glue wheel
- » Ruler
- » Bone folder

Method

1. Copy the template on p. 188.
2. Score the cardstock along all the straight lines.
3. Paste the white cardstock inside the square section of the card. You will write or print the message here.
4. Fold the round edges over each other as indicated.
5. Colour the edges of the paper flowers using the silver pen.
6. Paste the flowers over one another and stick them in the centre of the card.
7. Use a glue dot to secure the silver-grey pearl as a finishing touch.

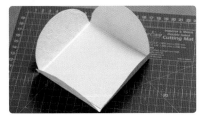 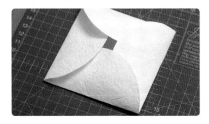 

Diagonal double fold

This fold is exceptionally suitable for scrapbook paper. Scrapbook paper often has beautiful designs on both sides, and it is such a pity when it has to be pasted onto other paper. This fold enables you to display both lovely sides of the paper. It is not a card that one would unfold; it acts as a double folder into which pretty labels containing messages can be inserted instead.

YOU WILL NEED

» Paper with patterns on both sides: A4 size (± 21 cm x 30 cm)
» Matching patterned paper (It can also be the same paper)
» Label punch
» Double-sided tape
» Pair of scissors or a guillotine
» Ruler
» Bone folder

Method

1. Score and fold the paper in half diagonally along the scored line.
2. Score and fold it across the length along the scored line.
3. Unfold the paper and cut along the horizontal fold until you reach the fold across the length of the paper.
4. Fold the bottom corner towards the right until the bottom edge of the paper is lined up against the centre fold line.
5. Fold the left-side corner towards the centre, but not up to the centre line. Leave approximately 3,5 cm between the fold and the centre line.
6. Fold the right angle across to the right-hand side.
7. Fold the right angle on the lower left-hand side in under the folded right angle on the right-hand side.
8. Fold the bottom right corner over the already folded corner of the other rectangle.
9. Fold the bottom half towards the top and glue at the top and the base.
10. Use the patterned paper to punch labels and place them inside the folders.

MAY ALL
YOUR
DREAMS
COME TRUE

Diamond fold

Even though this fold may appear to be complicated, it is actually very easy as long as you follow the steps exactly.

YOU WILL NEED

» Purple cardstock:
  10 cm x 30 cm
» 2 pieces of patterned paper:
  4,5 cm x 9,5 cm
» Split pin
» Acetate
» Patterned paper:
  6,5 cm x 6,5 cm
» Purple paper:
  6,5 cm x 6,5 cm
» Glue pen
» Glue wheel
» Ruler
» Bone folder

Method

1. Mark the middle of the purple cardstock with a pencil. DO NOT fold.
2. Fold the right-hand side of the paper towards the middle – until the side meets the pencil line and repeat on the left.
3. Unfold the paper and repeat steps 2 and 3 in the opposite direction. Open all the folds.
4. Now fold the right-hand side of the paper toward the inside, up to where the previous fold lines cross each other. Unfold and do the same with the left-hand side of the paper.
5. Unfold and fold the left- and right-hand sides towards the inside, 5 cm from the sides.
6. Press the diamond folds together to make the diamond shape.
7. Paste the patterned paper on the 5 cm pieces along the sides.
8. Prepare the section that will contain the message as follows:
   • Use your computer to print on the acetate. Make sure that you use the correct acetate for your printer.
   • Cut the acetate and paste it on the edge of the patterned paper using the glue pen.
   • Cut a small frame of purple patterned paper and paste the frame on the acetate and attach to the front of the card.

Folded circular card

This card is quite popular among brides-to-be because, thanks to the embellishments, it is unique. Adapt the colours to suit your fancy and to give it a personal feel.

YOU WILL NEED

» White pearlescent cardstock: A4 size
» Purple cardstock: 18 cm x 8 cm
» Purple cardstock: 17 cm x 6 cm
» Purple skeleton leaf
» Purple paper roses
» Purple organza ribbon: 10 cm long and 1 cm wide
» Glue wheel
» Glue dots
» Pair of compasses
» Ruler
» Bone folder

Method

1. Use the pair of compasses or a round object of the same size to draw a circle that is 21 cm in diameter.
2. Score and fold an 8 cm panel towards the inside along the scored line.
3. Fold another 5 cm panel towards the inside of circle from the opposite side.
4. Cut purple inlays that are slightly larger than the folded panels and paste these on the inside of each panel.
5. Use the ribbon to make a bow and paste it, together with the skeleton leaf and paper rose, in the centre of the card.

Flagged-fold card

Because we are a large family, we often contribute towards buying one big gift for a family member. And we usually want to give that special member of our family a card that represents all of us. This card is ideally suited for such an occasion, because you can paste as many "flags" as you wish into it. Everyone who wishes to do so uses a flag to write a personal message.

YOU WILL NEED

» Black cardstock: A4 size
» Black and white patterned paper: 8,5 cm x 19,5 cm
» 9 black and white frames: different sizes
» White cardstock to paste inside the frames
» Glue
» Ruler
» Bone folder

Method

1. Score and fold the A4 size cardstock in half along the width of the card (it is reduced to A5 size).
2. Score and fold another three folds, each 2 cm from the previous one, on both sides of the centre fold.
3. Fold lines on alternate sides of the card so that the card can fold into a concertina shape.
4. Prepare the flags by sticking the paper to the reverse side of the frames.
5. Paste the frames inside the card on the various folds.
6. Decorate the front of the card with patterned paper and tie a ribbon around it.

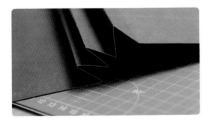

The panels of the black and white card
are decorated using various types
of patterned paper and the matting
technique on p. 15.

Tri-fold shutter card

This card derives its name from the fact that it is made up of various panels after you have folded and cut it. You can decide how many of the panels you want to decorate. If you want to keep it simple, decorate some of the panels. If you prefer intricate details, decorate all of them.

YOU WILL NEED

» White cardstock:
  27 cm x 14 cm
» 2 pieces of white and
  red dotted paper:
  13,5 cm x 4 cm each
» 3 different heart craft
  punches
» Patterned paper for the hearts
» Red and white dotted ribbon:
  10 cm
» Acetate on which to print
» Glue pen
» Ruler
» Bone folder
» Craft knife

Method

1. Score the white cardstock at 4,5 cm, 9 cm, 18 cm and 22,5 cm.
2. Fold the scored panels towards the inside and outside alternately.
3. Use the craft knife and the steel ruler to measure and cut 4 cm off the top edge between the two side panels.
4. Repeat step 3, but cut 4 cm from the base of the card.
5. As for the centre panel of the card, fold the crease lines in the opposite directions.
6. Print the message on acetate and punch it using the heart craft punch.
7. Paste the message on a punched white cardstock heart of the same size.
8. Punch a red edge using the heart craft punch and paste it on the message.
9. Decorate the outer panels with red and white dotted paper and punch more hearts in the other panels.
10. Use the ribbon to decorate the bottom panel.

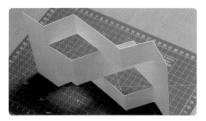

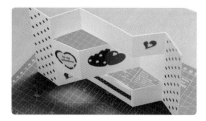

Craft punching

While I am watching television, I often punch out various shapes using scrap paper and craft punches; then I always have shapes handy should I quickly want to make a card. Unless it is really necessary, I do not punch cardstock. The shapes are usually pasted onto cardstock, so I simply used paper for the punching.

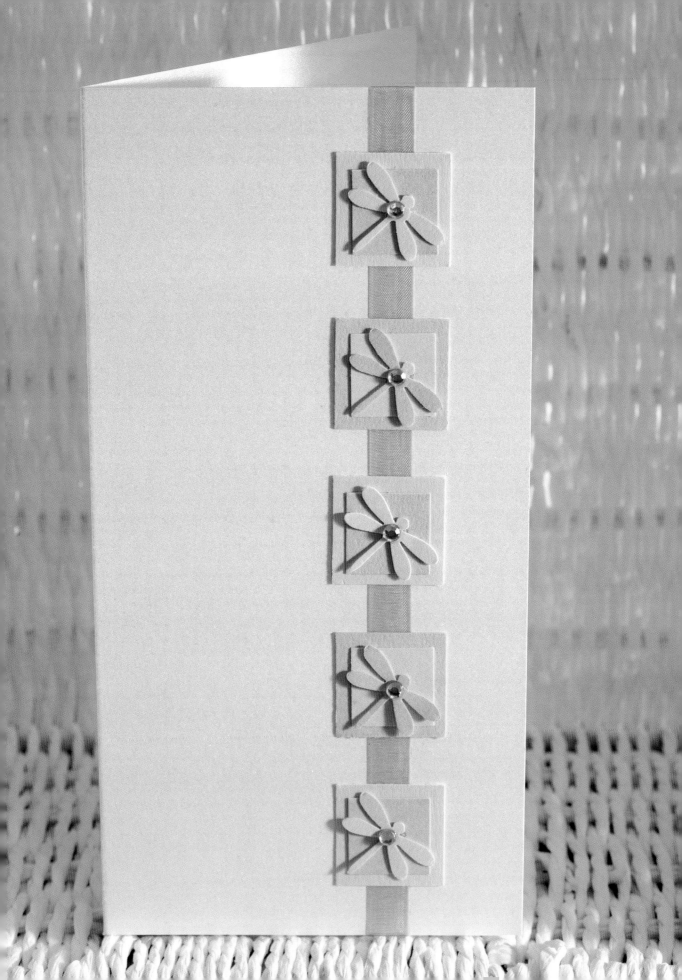

Pink and green dragonflies

To make this card, I used a dragonfly craft punch and two square punches of different sizes.

YOU WILL NEED

» White pearlescent cardstock:
  20 cm x 20 cm
» Pink organza ribbon:
  25 cm long and 1 cm wide
» Green and pink paper or
  cardstock to punch the
  squares and dragonflies
» 5 small, round rhinestones
» Dragonfly craft punch
» Square punch (2 sizes)
» Double-sided tape
» Glue pen
» Ruler
» Bone folder

Method

1. Score and fold the white pearlescent cardstock in half along the scored line to make the card.
2. Use the square punches and cut three large and two small green squares.
3. Punch out two large and three small pink squares.
4. Punch three green and two pink dragonflies.
5. Prepare the five squares by mounting a small square and a dragonfly on a big square. Vary the colours.
6. Use a glue pen to paste a rhinestone on each dragonfly.
7. Use a strip of double-sided tape to stick the ribbon down 3 cm from the edge of the card.
8. Stick the five squares over the ribbon, spacing them evenly along the side of the card.

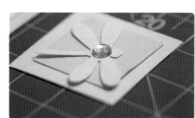

Glittering snowflakes

The simplicity of this card contributes towards its beauty. I used only a snowflake craft punch, and played around with rhinestones and silver sticky tape.

YOU WILL NEED

» Silver pearlescent cardstock:
  20 cm x 10 cm
» White pearlescent paper for
  the snowflakes
» 8 round rhinestones
» Snowflake craft punch
» Glue pen
» Silver sticky tape
» Ruler
» Bone folder

Method

1. Score and fold the silver pearlescent cardstock in half along the scored line to make the card.
2. Punch eight snowflakes from the white pearlescent paper.
3. Use the glue pen and paste the snowflakes on the card in the shape of an octahedron. Apply glue only to the centre of the snowflakes.
4. Use the glue pen to paste a rhinestone in the centre of each snowflake.
5. Finish off by pasting the silver sticky tape around the edges of the card.

Elegant silver heart

The paper and the heart craft punch make this card so exceptional, it may very well be used as a wedding invitation.

YOU WILL NEED

» White pearlescent cardstock: 29 cm x 11 cm
» 2 pieces of silver cardstock: 11 cm x 3 cm each
» Silver and white patterned paper to punch the heart
» Silver ribbon: 32 cm long and 1,5 cm wide
» Double-sided tape
» Glue pen
» Ruler
» Bone folder

Method

1. Score and fold the white pearlescent card-stock in half along the scored line to make the card.
2. Use the double-sided tape to attach the ribbon 2,5 cm from the lower edge of the greeting card.
3. Paste the silver cardstock on the inside of the card to cover the ribbon that has been folded over to that side.
4. Punch two hearts from the patterned paper and paste these on the ribbon as shown.

Make this cute little lamb with punched flowers and hearts.
I used a pair of scissors to cut out the face, and for the ears I used two halves of a heart. The legs are four thin, elongated strips that I cut with a pair of scissors.

Little lamb

YOU WILL NEED

» Blue cardstock: 24 cm x 12 cm
» Blue paper with dots or any other pattern:
  11 cm x 11 cm
» White pearlescent paper for the lamb's flowers
  and hearts
» Light grey pearlescent paper for the face
  and ears
» Flower craft punch
» Heart craft punch
» Glue pen
» Double-sided tape
» Ruler
» Bone folder

Method

1. Score and fold the blue cardstock in half along the scored line to make the card.
2. Cut the blue patterned paper to create a 1 cm frame.
3. Stick the frame in position on the front of the card.
4. Punch eleven flowers and six hearts from the white paper.
5. Cut the face and ears from the grey paper.
6. Start by pasting all the hearts on the lower edge of the card. Insert them slightly underneath the patterned frame.
7. Shape the lamb with the ten flowers and use the glue pen to stick each one to the card separately.
8. Paste the face and ears, followed by the last white flower.
9. Lastly, attach the legs.
10. If you prefer not to use paper strips for the legs, you can use a white pen to draw them on the card.

Benny Bookworm

YOU WILL NEED

- » Green cardstock: 20 cm x 20 cm
- » White cardstock: 19 cm x 9 cm
- » Scrap pieces of various green patterned papers
- » Red patterned paper
- » Pink paper
- » 2 googly eyes
- » Circle craft punch
- » Flower craft punch
- » Glue wheel
- » Glue pen
- » Ruler
- » Bone folder
- » Black pen

This card is ridiculously easy to make, but it is still very cute and sure to excite any child. I used only circles that I punched from patterned paper in various shades of green. Even the hat is half a circle. If you do not have a flower craft punch like the one I used on the hat, you can simply draw the flower. The googly eyes add a nice finishing touch.

Use a smaller circle craft punch if you want to make a smaller worm.

Method

1. Score and fold the green cardstock in half along the scored line to make the card.
2. Mount the white cardstock on the green card using a glue wheel.
3. Punch eight circles from the green patterned paper and paste them on the white card to shape the worm.
4. Punch out a red circle, cut it in half and paste it on the last green circle to make the hat.
5. Punch two flowers from the pink paper.
6. Draw the legs as well as a mouth of the worm, and stems for the flowers.
7. Use the glue pen to paste the flowers and the googly eyes into position.

MORE IDEAS

CARDS USING BORDER PUNCHES

Border punches add a lovely finish touch to any card, and sometimes it is exactly what you need to turn an ordinary card into a very special creation. Many border punches shape beautiful edges, but you can also use the punched out shapes.

Card with ribbon

YOU WILL NEED

» White pearlescent cardstock: 20 cm x 9 cm
» Sturdy red paper (not cardstock): 10 cm x 9 cm
» 6 paste-on pearls
» White organza ribbon:
   11 cm long and 5 mm wide
» Floral border punch
» Double-sided tape
» Glue pen
» Ruler
» Bone folder

Method

1. Score and fold the white cardstock in half along the scored line to make the card.
2. Use the border punch to make a design along one of the short sides of the red paper.
3. Stick the ribbon onto the red paper, approximately 5 mm above the punched design, using double-sided tape.
4. Use the glue pen to attach the pearls to the ribbon.
5. Paste the red paper on the white cardstock, leaving a 1 cm white strip to show.
6. Keep the punched-out red flowers. They are going to be used to complete the next card, as well as the one on p. 120.

Without ribbon

YOU WILL NEED

» Sturdy red paper: 20 cm x 10 cm
» White paper: 12 cm x 3 cm
» 6 paste-on pearls
» Red punched flowers (left over from previous card)
» Floral border punch
» Glue pen
» Ruler
» Bone folder

Method

1. Score and fold the red paper in half along the scored line to make the card.
2. Use the floral border punch to make a design on both edges of the white paper.
3. Use the glue pen to stick the red flowers between the punched white flowers.
4. Paste the pearls on the red flowers.
5. Mount the white strip on the sturdy red paper, approximately 2,5 cm from the edge, on the front of the card.

Rubber stamping

I remember very well how extremely popular rubber stamps were a few years ago, when more and more people started making their own cards. Since then, the technique has continued to grow and the variety of stamps and inks available today is astonishing. I have many rubber stamps that are mounted on wood and work perfectly well. The see-through stamps available these days make stamping so much easier since you can see exactly where you are placing the design, while the wood-block ones leave you guessing.

Today some stamps are manufactured using laser technology and, as a result, the detail is extremely fine and precise.

Masking technique for stamping

When you use white embossing powder, you can achieve interesting masking effects. It looks especially striking when a word stamp is used, as the example illustrates. A stamp with sheet music and notes also looks lovely.

YOU WILL NEED

» Brown pearlescent cardstock: 22 cm x 16,5 cm
» Patterned paper that matches the cardstock: 15,5 cm x 10,5 cm
» White glossy cardstock: 14 cm x 9,5 cm
» Rubber stamp: word
» Inkpad: colourless and walnut-brown
» Rubber roller
» White embossing powder
» Heat-gun
» Double-sided tape
» Ruler
» Bone folder

Method

1. Score and fold the brown cardstock in half along the scored line to make the card.
2. Press the stamp onto the colourless inkpad.
3. Press the ink-covered stamp on the glossy card.
4. Sprinkle embossing powder over the design.
5. Heat the embossing powder carefully until it has melted. Do not hold the heat-gun too close to the paper.
6. Roll the rubber roller over the walnut inkpad and then over the stamped cardstock.
7. Use a tissue to wipe the ink from the design – the ink will be rubbed in between the embossed image.
8. Cut this cardstock smaller and use double-sided tape to paste it, as well as the patterned paper, onto the front of the card using the matting technique (refer to p. 15).
9. This technique looks equally beautiful if you use other colour combinations.

Dog and trailer filled with love

This stamp was one of the first that I bought somewhere between 1980 and 1990. I remember all too well how I used it to make Valentine's Day cards. It is still one of my favourite stamps.

YOU WILL NEED

» White glossy cardstock: 21 cm x 15 cm
» Black cardstock: 10 cm x 9 cm
» Silver pearlescent cardstock: 8,5 cm x 7,5 cm
» Red cardstock: 7,5 cm x 6,5 cm
» White cardstock: 6,5 cm x 5,5 cm
» Rubber stamp: dog
» Black pigment inkpad
» Neutral embossing powder
» 17 red heart-shaped gemstones
» Double-sided tape
» Glue pen
» Heat-gun
» Ruler
» Bone folder

Method

1. Press the dog stamp on the black inkpad and stamp the design onto the small piece of white cardstock.
2. Sprinkle embossing powder over the design. Shake off the excess powder carefully and collect it in the container.
3. Heat the embossing powder using the heat-gun as described on p. 14.
4. Use the glue pen to paste the red heart-shaped gemstones on the stamped hearts.
5. Score and fold the white cardstock in half along the scored line to make the card.
6. Use double-sided tape to paste the black, silver, red and white cardstock onto the front of the card, using the matting technique as described on p. 15.
7. Should you wish to use this design to make a card, you can copy the template on p. 189. However, you will not be able to emboss it.

Pink heart

YOU WILL NEED

- » White glossy cardstock: 15 cm x 10,5 cm
- » Rubber stamp: heart
- » Bright pink embossing powder
- » Heat-gun
- » Organza ribbon: pink with white dots, 12 cm
- » Double-sided tape
- » Inkpad: pink or colourless
- » Ruler
- » Bone folder

Method

1. Score and fold the white cardstock in half along the scored line to make the card.
2. Stamp the heart on the front of the card and sprinkle embossing powder over it.
3. Use the heat-gun to heat the embossing powder until it has melted.
4. Stick the ribbon 5 mm from the base of the card using double-sided tape.

Pink lips

YOU WILL NEED

» Black cardstock: 29 cm x 11,5 cm
» Bright pink cardstock with circles and edge
» Rubber stamp: lips
» Colourless or pink inkpad
» Bright pink embossing powder
» Heat-gun
» Circle craft punch: medium and small
» Double-sided tape
» Ruler
» Bone folder

Method

1. Score and fold the black cardstock in half along the scored line to make the card.
2. Punch three medium pink circles.
3. Punch three smaller black circles.
4. Stamp lips on the small black circles and sprinkle embossing powder over the designs.
5. Heat the embossing powder with the heat-gun until it has melted.
6. Paste a pink border onto the black card and paste a 5 mm strip of pink cardstock 2,5 cm from the base of the card.
7. Glue the black circles onto the pink circles and paste them on the card as shown.

These two cards were stamped in black and then embossed using colourless embossing powder. Afterwards they were decorated with glitter glue and flowers.

Simply white

YOU WILL NEED

» White cardstock: large enough for the stamps that you are going to use
» Black inkpad
» Rubber stamp of your choice
» Colourless embossing powder
» Heat-gun
» Glitter glue: various colours
» Punched shapes, e.g. flowers
» Ruler
» Bone folder

Method

1. Cut and fold white cards that match the size of the stamps.
2. Stamp the design in black and emboss using the colourless embossing powder.
3. Use the glitter glue or punched shapes, such as flowers, to decorate the card.
4. If you are not using these specific stamps, you can copy the templates on p. 189 for your cards.

Quilling (paper filigree)

Quilling or paper filigree is an ancient art that involves the rolling and shaping of thin paper strips. Delicate coils and scrolls can be joined together to create various three-dimensional designs. Some of my friends are avid quillers and they have convinced me that it can be addictive. Lynette created the beautiful cards in this chapter. Some of the designs that she has used are available on the Internet and may be downloaded free of charge.

See www.whimsiquills.com

I really enjoy quilling too, because one can create something unique using only a few basic techniques. The only disadvantage is the delicacy of the coils and scrolls. One has to handle these cards with extreme care, and be careful not to allow heavy objects to fall on the work and squash it.

The basic filigree shapes are created with a thin strip of paper that is gently rolled around a quilling tool. The paper strips are available in various widths – the most commonly used papers are 3 mm or 6 mm wide. The purpose of this book is not to discuss all the techniques in detail, but rather to provide a few paper filigree ideas for you to use.

The basic shapes used in quilling are shown on the opposite page.

BASIC SHAPES USED IN QUILLING

Tight/closed coil

Roll a coil and glue the end down while still on the tool.

Loose coil

Roll a coil and remove it from the tool. Let it expand a little before gluing down the paper end.

Teardrop

Roll a loose coil, pinch one side and leave the other round.

Marquise/eye

Roll a loose coil and pinch opposite ends.

Half moon

Roll a loose coil, and glue and pinch opposite ends. Then shape the moon around the tool.

C-scroll

Roll each end of the paper towards the middle of the strip.

S-scroll

Roll each end towards the middle from opposite ends of the paper. Then curve into an "S" shape.

V-scroll

Fold the paper in half and roll each end outwards.

Heart scroll

Fold the paper in half and roll each end inwards.

One-sided V-scroll

Fold the paper in half, then roll each end in the same direction.

Ring coil

Roll a tight/closed coil, but use the handle of the tool.

Pressed heart

Roll a loose coil, then pinch one end into a point and indent the other side with your fingernail, making a heart shape.

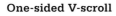

Basket of flowers

This basket is made from a combination of most of the basic shapes. The beautiful little flowers make it really special. All the paper strips are 3 mm wide.

YOU WILL NEED

The working length of each coil is indicated following the colour and coil/scroll shape.

For the card:

» Purple cardstock:
22 cm x 13 cm
» Dark purple pearlescent
cardstock: 11 cm x 9 cm
» Light purple pearlescent
cardstock: 10 cm x 8 cm
» Glue wheel
» Craft glue
» Toothpick
» Ruler
» Bone folder

For the basket:

» 2 light brown C-scrolls: 8 cm
» 5 light brown marquise coils:
8 cm
» 6 light brown teardrops: 8 cm
» 12 light brown marquise
coils: 4 cm

(continued on next page)

Method

1. Complete all the separate filigree shapes before you start putting them onto the card. Arrange and paste the completed shapes together as shown in the diagram below.
2. Score and fold the purple cardstock in half along the scored line to make the card.
3. Paste the dark purple and light purple cardstock on the front of the card using the glue wheel.
4. Use craft glue and a toothpick to stick the basket and flowers on the card as shown.

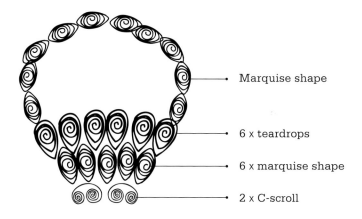

Marquise shape

6 x teardrops

6 x marquise shape

2 x C-scroll

For the blue flower:

» 7 light blue teardrops: 4 cm
» 1 yellow tight/closed coil:
  4 cm
» 1 green marquise coil: 4 cm

For the light pink flower:

» 5 pink ring coils: 8 cm
» 1 yellow tight/closed coil:
  4 cm
» 1 green marquise coil: 8 cm

For the dark pink flower:

» 5 pink teardrops: 4 cm
» 1 green teardrop: 4 cm
» 1 green tight/closed coil: 4 cm

For the yellow flower:

» 4 yellow hearts: 8 cm

For the rosebud under the basket:

» 1 pink teardrop: 8 cm
» 1 green V-scroll: 8 cm
» 2 green marquise coils: 4 cm

Wild ducks on spun silk

The ducks look stunning on the silkworm-spun oval. Didn't we all keep silkworms when we were young? Lynette has quite a number of these spun shapes dating back to the days of her son's silkworm business!

YOU WILL NEED

For the card:

» Brown cardstock: 20 cm x 15 cm
» 1 spun shape – oval
» Glue dots
» Craft glue
» Ruler
» Bone folder

For the wild ducks:

All the paper strips that are used for the ducks are 6 mm wide. To shape the head with the eye, you must attach the paper strips as follows: 1 cm black to 2 cm white and then to 30 cm dark green. Repeat this step for the smaller duck's head, but use only 20 cm green paper instead of 30 cm.

» 2 brown teardrops: 30 cm for the large duck and 20 cm for the small one
» Small pieces of red paper for the beaks

For the bulrushes, grass and reeds:

» The bulrushes are made of 3 mm strips – but make four tight coils for each bulrush and stitch it with a piece of florist wire.
» Shape the grass and reeds on the card as shown.

Method

1. Score and fold the brown cardstock in half along the scored line to make the card.
2. Paste the silk oval on the card using glue dots.
3. Use craft glue to stick the filigree shapes on the card as shown.

Brightly coloured flowers in windows

These pretty, brightly coloured kaleidoscope flowers are made with different shades of the same colour for each floral leaf. The various shades of paper are pasted together from light to dark. Sometimes you must start coiling at the light end and at other times you will start coiling at the dark end of the strip. The paper strips are all 3 mm wide.

YOU WILL NEED

For the card:

» Light brown cardstock: 24 cm x 12 cm
» Gold-coloured pearlescent cardstock: 11 cm x 11 cm
» Craft knife
» Double-sided tape
» Ruler
» Bone folder

For the filigree shapes:

» 3 orange/yellow teardrops (made of three shades of yellow/orange): 20 cm each
» 3 pink teardrops (made of three shades of pink): 20 cm each
» 3 green marquise coils (made of three shades of green): 20 cm
» 3 blue marquise coils (made of three shades of blue): 20 cm
» 4 dark green V-scrolls: 10 cm each

Method

1. Score and fold the light brown card in half along the scored line to make the card.
2. Cut four 4,5 cm x 4,5 cm windows in the front of the card. The edges of the windows are 1 cm wide.
3. Paste the gold-coloured cardstock inside the front panel of the card.
4. Arrange and paste the filigree shapes in the windows as shown, using craft glue.

You can paste two feet on the card instead of only one; you can also change the colour from pink to blue.

Pink foot

YOU WILL NEED

For the card:

- » Pink cardstock: 16 cm x 8 cm
- » White pearlescent card: 5 cm x 5 cm
- » Glue wheel
- » Ruler
- » Bone folder

For the foot (made of 3 mm-strips)

- » 5 pink tight coils: 4 of 20 cm and 1 of 25 cm
- » 2 pink teardrops: 25 cm
- » Craft glue
- » Toothpick

Method

1. Score and fold the pink cardstock in half along the scored line to make the card.
2. Paste the white cardstock diagonally on the pink card.
3. Use the toothpick and craft glue to paste the filigree shapes on the card.

Left: I received this card from my friend, Rowena. The letters are made of pewter and were embossed using a Cuttlebug™. They were then treated with patina and polished with metal polish. Stunning and original!

Marvellous metal

You do not only have to consider using cardstock and paper when you think of making cards. I love working with metal. You can shape it and, with little effort, a simple piece of metal can become the focal point of a card. I have used pewter and copper, as well as craft foil. Craft foil is available in a range of colours.

One does not need large pieces of foil or pewter to make a card special. The metal that I mention here can also be embossed using the Cuttlebug™ (see p. 86). Before I bought a Cuttlebug™, I used a pasta maker for the embossing. I put the embossing template and the metal through the rollers of the pasta maker and was really pleased with the results.

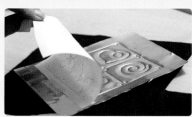

Reliable pewter

Pewter work is growing in popularity and, while you may have battled to get hold of some in the past, it is now readily available at most craft shops. The design that I have used for the card can also be used on a jewellery box or a cardholder. Follow all the steps for making the card, but paste the design on a container instead.

YOU WILL NEED

- » Silver pearlescent cardstock: 26 cm x 13 cm
- » Dark blue cardstock: 12 cm x 12 cm
- » Pewter: 15 cm x 15 cm
- » Embossing pen
- » Felt square
- » Cotton
- » Patina
- » Paper plate
- » Masking tape
- » Double-sided tape
- » Spirits
- » Ruler
- » Bone folder

Method

1. Copy the template on p. 190.
2. Tape the template to the pewter with masking tape.
3. Work on the felt square and trace the template onto the pewter. Use the embossing pen and press slightly harder than you would when you are writing.
4. Remove the template from the pewter.
5. Turn the pewter over and work on a hard surface.
6. Use the paper plate and trace the pattern on either side of the line that was drawn in step 3.
7. Wipe the entire piece of pewter with spirits to remove any oily stains.
8. Wear gloves and use cotton wool to wipe patina over the entire design. The design will turn black wherever the patina touches the metal.
9. Wipe off the excess patina using a paper towel.
10. Use a clean piece of cotton wool to apply the metal polish. Polish the design until it shines.
11. Score and fold the silver cardstock in half along the scored line to make the card. Paste the blue cardstock on the front with double-sided tape.
12. Cut the pewter design smaller and glue it to the blue cardstock using either pewter glue or double-sided tape.

Ethnic copper

Copper works as well as pewter, but it is not as soft. The colour of copper changes from reddish pink to shades of blue and white when it is heated with a heat-gun.

YOU WILL NEED

» Cream-coloured pearlescent cardstock: 20 cm x 20 cm
» Dark brown pearlescent cardstock: 18 cm x 7 cm
» Copper: 20 cm x 10 cm
» Heat-gun
» Embossing tool
» Felt square
» Masking tape
» Double-sided tape
» Ruler
» Bone folder

Method

1. Copy the template on p. 190.
2. Follow steps 2–6 as set out for Reliable pewter (p. 74–75).
3. Heat the copper below the template until the colour of the copper changes. It will take quite a while – just be patient.
4. You must work on a heat-resistant surface, since copper is a good conductor of heat and the surface can grow very hot.
5. Score and fold the cream-coloured cardstock in half along the scored line to make the card.
6. Paste the dark brown cardstock onto the front, using double-sided tape.
7. Cut the copper design smaller – approximately 6 cm x 17 cm – and stick it to the brown cardstock with double-sided tape.

Elegant metal flower

This card is really very simple to make, because I used the Cuttlebug™ to transfer this stunning flower onto metal. I used a Cuttlebug™ edge folder to transfer the design onto craft foil. This card is an excellent example of matting that is discussed on p. 15. Each consecutive layer of the card is approximately 5 mm smaller than the preceding one.

YOU WILL NEED

» Cream-coloured pearlescent cardstock: 20 cm x 20 cm
» Dark brown pearlescent cardstock: 16 cm x 5,5 cm
» Light brown pearlescent cardstock: 15 cm x 4,5 cm
» Light blue pearlescent cardstock: 14 cm x 3,5 cm
» Craft foil: 13 cm x 2,5 cm
» Cuttlebug™
» Edge folder: floral template
» Double-sided tape
» Ruler
» Bone folder

Method

1. Use the Cuttlebug™ template and pass the edge folder containing the foil through the Cuttlebug™.
2. Score and fold the cream-coloured cardstock in half along the scored line to make the card.
3. Use double-sided tape and paste the rest of the card strips onto the front of the card using the matting technique discussed on p. 15.
4. Stick the foil onto the blue cardstock.

Funky metal hearts

YOU WILL NEED

- » Black cardstock: 20 cm x 15 cm
- » Silver cardstock: 12 cm x 9,5 cm
- » Pink metal gauze: 12 cm x 9,5 cm
- » 3 metal hearts
- » Cuttlebug™
- » Gold metallic embroidery thread
- » Craft knife
- » Double-sided tape
- » Glue dots
- » Heart craft punch
- » Ruler
- » Bone folder

The hearts on this card are also made of ordinary craft foil in various colours. Typical crafter that I am, I spotted this pink metallic gauze at a sale and bought a whole roll. I just knew I would find a use for it some day. If you do not have anything similar, you can punch holes in craft foil. You can also use chicken wire or any other wire gauze.

Method

1. Punch out three hearts of different colours using the craft punch.
2. Put each heart into a separate Cuttlebug™ embossing folder and emboss it.
3. Use the gold embroidery thread to attach the hearts to the metal gauze. Secure the thread on the reverse side using glue dots.
4. Score and fold the black cardstock in half along the scored line to make the card.
5. Use a craft knife to cut a 10,5 cm x 8 cm window in the silver cardstock.
6. Paste the silver frame over the pink metal gauze and stick everything onto the front of the card using double-sided tape.

Paste and rub

YOU WILL NEED

» White cardstock: 21 cm x 13 cm
» Red cardstock: 10 cm x 10 cm
» Scrap cardstock: 9 cm x 9 cm
» Craft foil: 10 cm x 10 cm
» Very thick chipboard shapes
» Craft glue
» Double-sided tape
» Cuttlebug™
» Ruler
» Bone folder

Making this card involves an exceptionally interesting technique. Pre-purchased or handmade designs are pasted onto an ordinary piece of cardstock. Craft foil is then placed over them and the surface is rubbed to make the designs stand out. You could also use very thick kitchen foil – the kind that is used by caterers. It still tears easily, so if you are going to use it, you will have to work very carefully.

Method

1. Paste the chipboard shapes on the scrap cardstock and make sure that the glue has dried completely before you start working with the foil.
2. Place the foil over the designs and, working from the centre, rub over the designs using a bone folder to make them stand out. Make sure to rub thoroughly around the edges of the shapes.
3. When you are satisfied with the design, fold the excess foil over the sides of the scrap cardstock and attach it using double-sided tape.
4. Score and fold the white cardstock in half along the scored line to make the card.
5. Emboss the front of the card using the Cuttlebug™.
6. Paste the red card and foil design onto the front of the card using the matting technique on p. 15.

Embossing

I have always considered embossed cards to be both beautiful and elegant. I love classic cards, especially ones made in a single colour. Nowadays you will find many embossing machines that will enable you to create the most spectacular backgrounds on which to work. Embossing can also be done using a light-box, and there is a wide variety of stencils that are suitable for this purpose. Stencils that contain intricate details are usually made of metal, but plastic stencils are also readily available.

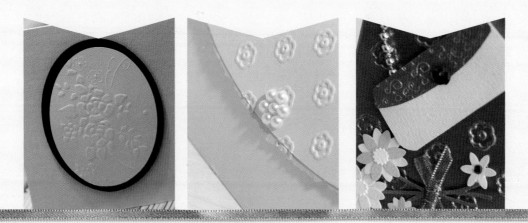

EMBOSSING USING A LIGHT-BOX

I have a big, clumsy old light-box, but it works perfectly. Smaller, more compact light-boxes are available. If you want to do embossing work, but do not have a light-box, you can work against a window through which light is shining. Working during broad daylight is obviously the best option.

Elegant purple embossed card

I made this card on the light-box, using a plastic stencil for the embossing work. You can use an ordinary embossing pen, but I have recently discovered a Teflon embossing tool that makes the task so much easier. The Teflon tool simply glides over the paper and it is just much more pleasant to use.

YOU WILL NEED

- » Dark brown pearlescent cardstock: 28 cm x 14 cm
- » 2 pieces of light purple pearlescent cardstock: 14 cm x 14 cm each
- » White organza ribbon: 50 cm long and 1 cm wide
- » Embossing pen/tool
- » Stencil
- » Light-box
- » Masking tape
- » Glue
- » Ruler
- » Bone folder

Method

1. Tape the stencil on the light-box using masking tape.
2. Tape one of the purple cardstock pieces over the stencil using masking tape.
3. Turn on the light-box and emboss the design using the embossing tool.
4. Once you have embossed the entire design, turn off the light-box and remove the cardstock and stencil.
5. Score and fold the dark-brown cardstock in half along the scored line to create the card.
6. Cut the light purple cardstock slightly smaller and stick the embossed motifs on the front of the card.
7. Attach the other purple cardstock to the inside of the card.
8. Tie the ribbon in the fold of the card and make a bow on the outside.

Delicate roses

Method

1. Score cream-coloured cardstock (17 cm x 7,5 cm) and fold in half along the scored line to make the card.
2. Emboss the design on the same colour cardstock – cut an oval shape.
3. Mount on a dark brown oval that is slightly larger.
4. Attach using foam tape to add dimension.

Silver spirals and stars

Method

1. Score white pearlescent cardstock (21 cm x 10,5 cm) and fold the cardstock in half along the scored line to create the card.
2. Emboss the design on white card.
3. Mount aslant on grey pearlescent cardstock and paste on the white greeting card.
4. Use silver glitter-glue for a fine finish.

Elegant rose

Method

1. Score light purple cardstock (15 cm x 6 cm) and fold in half along the scored line to make the card.
2. Emboss the design directly on the cardstock.
3. Paste a piece of white cardstock inside the card.

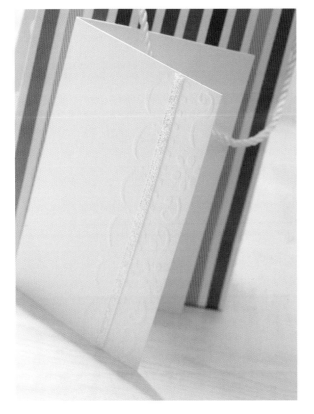

Soft and simple edge

Method

1. Score light yellow cardstock (20 cm x 15 cm) and fold in half along the scored line to make the card.
2. Emboss the design directly on the cardstock.
3. Finish using pearlescent ribbon.

EMBOSSING USING A CUTTLEBUG™

This little machine will provide beautifully embossed backgrounds in next to no time. You need special folders into which the cardstock or paper that you wish to emboss is inserted before it is passed through the Cuttlebug™. You can also use this machine to emboss metals such as aluminium foil or pewter.

Pink card with white flower

YOU WILL NEED

» Dark pink cardstock: 21 cm x 11 cm
» 2 large white paper flowers
» 1 small pink button
» Self-adhesive paper ribbon: 12 cm
» Ruler
» Bone folder
» Glue
» Cuttlebug™

Method

1. Score and then fold the pink cardstock in half along the scored line.
2. Emboss the front using the Cuttlebug™.
3. Stick the paper ribbon along the base of the card, about 1,5 cm from the edge.
4. Paste the two white flowers together and stick them in the centre of the card.
5. Stick the button in the centre of the flowers.

Pink tulip card

YOU WILL NEED

» White cardstock: 16 cm x 12 cm
» Pink pearlescent cardstock: 11 cm x 7 cm
» Handmade sticker
» Glue
» Ruler
» Bone folder
» Cuttlebug™

Method

1. Score and then fold the white cardstock in half along the scored line to make the card.
2. Emboss the pink cardstock with the Cuttlebug™.
3. Paste the handmade sticker in the centre of the card, at the base.

Bronze handbag

YOU WILL NEED

» Bronze pearlescent cardstock: 12 cm x 8 cm
» Handmade stickers: handbag and flowers
» Glue
» Ruler
» Bone folder
» Cuttlebug™

Method

1. Score and fold the bronze cardstock in half along the scored line.
2. Emboss the front of the card using the Cuttlebug™.
3. Paste the handmade stickers on the card.

Purple rabbit-card

YOU WILL NEED

» Light-purple cardstock: 18 cm x 15 cm
» Patterned paper that matches the cardstock:
   15 cm x 3,3 cm
» Pearlescent ribbon: 15 cm
» 2 purple split pins
» Handmade rabbit sticker
» Ruler
» Bone folder
» Cuttlebug™

Method

1. Score and fold the purple cardstock in half along the scored line.
2. Emboss the front of the card using the Cuttlebug™.
3. Use a pair of deckle-edged craft scissors to cut a wavy pattern along one of the long sides of the patterned paper. Paste the paper, together with the pearlescent ribbon, against the left-hand side of the card.
4. Stick the rabbit sticker and miniature label on the card.
5. Fix one split pin to the top left-hand side, and the other to the bottom left-hand side of the card.

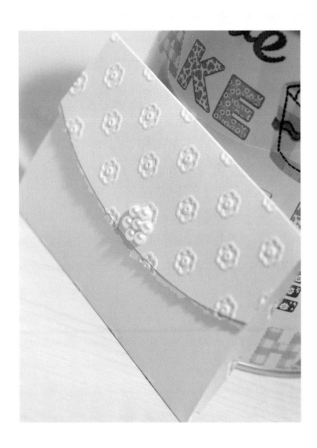

White handbag card

YOU WILL NEED

» White cardstock: 18 cm x 11 cm
» Pink cardstock: 11 cm x 4,5 cm
» 7 pearl-coloured paste-on pearls
» Glue
» Ruler
» Bone folder
» Cuttlebug™

Method

1. Score the white cardstock at 6,5 cm and 14 cm.
2. Fold in along the scored line.
3. Cut the smallest panel of the white cardstock in the shape of a curve.
4. Paste the pink cardstock on the inside panel. Use the deckle-edged craft scissors to cut the pink cardstock so that it is slightly larger than the white cardstock. Fold this panel over the bottom one so that it resembles a handbag.
5. Use the Cuttlebug™ to emboss only the top flap of the handbag.
6. Stick the seven pearls on the card to resemble the clasp.

Ballet shoe card

YOU WILL NEED

» Black pearlescent cardstock: 16 cm x 7 cm
» Light-purple pearlescent cardstock:
  7 cm x 6 cm
» Black card: 3,5 cm x 3,5 cm
» Ballet-shoe stamp
» Inkpad
» Colourless embossing powder
» Heat-gun
» Glue
» Rule
» Bone folder
» Cuttlebug™

Method

1. Score and fold the black pearl cardstock in half along the scored line.
2. Emboss the light-purple cardstock using the Cuttlebug™.
3. Press the ballet shoe stamp onto the ink-pad and stamp the picture onto the small black square.
4. Sprinkle embossing powder over the picture and heat using the heat-gun.
5. Paste the embossed cardstock on the front of the card, and also paste the ballet shoe in the corner of the card.

Card with treble clef and red ribbon

YOU WILL NEED

- » White cardstock: 18 cm × 10 cm
- » Black pearlescent cardstock: 6,5 cm × 7 cm
- » Bronze corrugated cardstock: 6 cm × 6 cm
- » Treble clef of gold-coloured metal
- » Small red bow
- » Scrap patterned paper on which music notes are printed
- » Matches
- » Glue
- » Ruler
- » Bone folder
- » Cuttlebug™

Method

1. Score and fold the white cardstock in half along the scored line.
2. Emboss the front of the card using the Cuttlebug™.
3. Burn the edges of the music paper using a match.
4. Paste the black cardstock onto the greeting card, followed by the corrugated cardstock, music paper, the treble clef and the red bow.

Cream-and-green embossed card

YOU WILL NEED

» Cardstock with a green and a cream-coloured side: 20 cm x 14 cm
» Cream-coloured cardstock: 8 cm x 13 cm
» Glue
» Ruler
» Bone folder
» Cuttlebug™

Method

1. Score and fold the green and cream-coloured cardstock so that the green side is on the outside. Do not fold it exactly in half, but allow a 2 cm strip of the cream to show.
2. Emboss the cream-coloured edge using the Cuttlebug™. Use one of the folders for the edges.
3. Emboss the cream-coloured cardstock using the Cuttlebug™. Paste this on the green card, leaving a green border around it.

Brown-and-black card

YOU WILL NEED

» Light brown cardstock: 21 cm x 15 cm
» Dark brown cardstock: 13 cm x 9 cm
» Black cardstock: 4 cm x 13 cm
» Glue
» Ruler
» Bone folder
» Cuttlebug™

Method

1. Score and fold the light brown cardstock in half along the scored line to make the greeting card.
2. Emboss the black cardstock using the Cuttlebug™. Use one of the folders for the edges.
3. Cut out the black cardstock along the edge of the embossed design and paste it on the dark brown cardstock.
4. Paste the dark brown cardstock on the front of the card.

Hints

» Light-weight paper yields the best results.
» If you use card, it is not necessary to fold it.
» Florist ribbon makes a good show and once folded;
  it has more depth.

Iris folding

I love patchwork and when I saw iris folding for the first time, it made me think of patchwork. What makes iris folding so much fun is finding suitable paper to use for your project. You can use various colours in one design, or one colour and various designs – exactly like patchwork. Iris folding originated in Holland, where early crafters used the insides of envelopes to make beautiful designs to use on cards. The name is derived from the appearance of the designs – it resembles the iris of the eye or camera. Nowadays any scrapbook paper, origami paper and even ribbon can be used for this paper art. I have used ordinary gift-wrap paper and even foil chocolate wrappers. You can use pages from magazines to create a whole new design.

Iris oval

For this card I used scraps of gold, silver and black paper left over after last Christmas. I am glad that I did not throw away the remaining bits, as they were perfect for this card.

YOU WILL NEED

» Black cardstock:
23 cm x 16 cm
» Silver cardstock:
10 cm x 15 cm (I usually start with a larger piece of card and later cut it to size.)
» 4 different types of patterned paper: silver, gold and black
» Sticky tape
» Double-sided tape
» Masking tape
» Corner punch
» Guillotine

Method

1. Copy the template on p. 191 and cut it out.
2. Tape it to a cutting mat with masking tape.
3. Cut an oval of silver cardstock and tape it on top of the iris pattern with masking tape.
4. Cut 2 cm strips of patterned paper. Fold back the edges 5 mm so that the strips are 1,5 cm wide.
5. Follow the design and glue the strips, placing the folded edges on the lines of the design.
6. Repeat the pattern until only a small opening is left – the "iris" of the design.
7. Remove the silver cardstock from the cutting mat and cut it to measure 10 cm x 15 cm.
8. Trim the corners with the corner punch.
9. Score and fold the black cardstock along the scored line to make the card.
10. Stick the iris design to the front of the card with double-sided tape.

Come dance with me

This iris fold design is made of foil chocolate wrap. Because foil folds are very flat, you have to fold the foil around a bit of card before pasting the strips.

YOU WILL NEED

» 2 pieces of cream-coloured pearlescent cardstock: 23 cm x 15 cm and 10 cm x 14 cm
» Scrap cardstock: 11 cm x 14,5 cm
» Black and red foil chocolate wrap
» Small black beads: 1 mm
» Round black Swarovski crystal: 4 mm
» Sticky tape
» Double-sided tape
» Masking tape
» Guillotine
» Glue pen

Method

1. Use the template on p. 191 and follow steps 1–6 of the Oval card (p. 97). Remember that you are using two colours of paper, not four.
2. Use the red and black strips as follows:
   • Red for 1–5 and 10, 11, 18, 21.
   • Black for 6–9, 13–17, 19, 20, 22.
3. Cut the cardstock on which the design is pasted smaller and use the glue pen to finish the top of the dress with beads and the Swarovski crystal.
4. Score and fold the large cream-coloured cardstock in half along the scored line.
5. Cover a piece of the scrap cardstock with foil chocolate wrap and stick it on top of the card. If you do not have enough black foil, you can simply paste it on the edge of the card and fold it over.
6. Stick the card with the iris design on top using double-sided tape.

The paper I used for this card is slightly thicker than ordinary gift-wrap or patterned paper. The bright colours make the card extraordinary. I have not folded the paper strips because the paper is too thick. Because it is equally bright on both sides, it does not have to be folded.

Brightly coloured flower card

YOU WILL NEED

» White cardstock: 24 cm x 14 cm
» Black cardstock: 11 cm x 13 cm
» Brightly coloured cardstock: 5 different colours
» Pieces of gold foil chocolate wrap for iris
» Masking tape
» Sticky tape
» Double-sided tape
» Guillotine
» Flower punch

Method

1. Use the template on p. 192 and follow steps 1–6 as set out for the Oval card (p. 97). The iris design is pasted on the black cardstock. Remember that you are using five colours of paper, not only four. You must not fold the strips of bright paper.
2. Stick the piece of gold foil chocolate wrap in the middle of the flower design.
3. Score and fold the white cardstock in half along the scored line to make the card.
4. Cut the black cardstock to size and glue it to the white card.
5. Use the brightly coloured cardstock to punch flowers and paste them in the corners as indicated.

Christmas balls

I also used foil chocolate wrap
to make these Christmas balls.
Because the colours that touch
each other are not the same, you
do not have to fold the foil around
card. You can change the colour as
you wish. I think this card would
also be pretty if you use traditional
Christmas colours – green, red
and gold.

YOU WILL NEED

- » 2 pieces of white cardstock: 20 cm x 18 cm
  and 9 cm x 17 cm
- » Silver, gold and purple foil chocolate wrap
- » Silver, gold and multi-coloured cord
- » Gold sticky tape
- » Masking tape
- » Sticky tape
- » Double-sided tape
- » Guillotine

Method

1. Copy the template on p. 193 and follow steps
   1–4 as set out for the Oval card (p. 97).
2. Please note that the colour strips in this case
   are not pasted alternately. Paste the same
   colour four times and start the next round
   with a new colour. Remove the masking tape
   and turn over the cardstock on which the
   design is pasted.
3. Cut the cord and stick it onto the card as
   illustrated. Make a bow of each cord colour
   and glue these too.
4. Score and fold the largest piece of white cardstock in half along the scored line to make
   the card.
5. Paste the cardstock that bears the iris
   design on the front of the card with double-
   sided tape.

The dark purple edge around the iris heart finishes the card beautifully. You can use traditional Valentine's Day colours – red, white and silver – to make the heart. It will also look pretty if the whole heart is red.

Iris heart

YOU WILL NEED

- » White pearlescent cardstock: 26 cm x 18 cm
- » Dark purple glossy cardstock: 12 cm x 17 cm
- » Light purple pearlescent cardstock:
  11 cm x 16 cm
- » Gold-coloured paper
- » Silver textured paper
- » White pearlescent paper
- » Dark purple chocolate foil
- » Sticky tape
- » Double-sided tape
- » Masking tape
- » Guillotine

Method

1. Copy the template on p. 192 and follow steps 1–6 of the Oval card (p. 97). You are now using three colours of paper and not four.
2. Paste a piece of dark purple chocolate foil in the iris of the pattern.
3. Mount the light purple cardstock on the dark purple.
4. Score and fold the white pearlescent cardstock in half along the scored line to make the card.
5. Stick the mounted iris design onto the front of the card with double-sided tape.

Teabag folding

Teabag folding is a paper folding art that originated in Europe. A Dutch lady, Tiny van der Plas, originally folded beautiful designs using the paper that had contained fruit-teabags – hence the name "teabag folding". The most basic folds are variations of a triangular and square fold. Once you have mastered the basic technique, you will be amazed by the many pattern variations into which the folded squares can be arranged to create a small work of art time and again.

Teabag folding squares are available on the Internet, so you can print them yourself. Downloading some for personal use is free, but most of the squares may not be distributed or used to make cards that are going to be sold. Always make sure of the copyright before using the squares to make a profit.

Most designs start with eight squares that are folded in a specific way and then arranged. The secret to teabag-folding success lies in accurate cutting and folding of the squares. Always work as precisely as possible when you fold these squares. There are two basic folds:

BASIC FOLD 1 (TRIANGULAR FOLD)

1. With the right side facing DOWN, fold the paper across from corner to corner to make a triangle.
2. Unfold and make the same fold across to the other corner. Unfold.
3. Turn the paper over so that the right side is facing UP, and fold the paper in half from top to bottom. Unfold.
4. Now fold it in half from left to right and unfold.
5. Push the paper towards the inside crease to create a triangle.
6. While keeping the double triangle flat, twist the right-hand side over to the left-hand side, and fold the left-hand bottom point of the triangle towards the centre.
7. Take the right side back again.
8. Do the same with the left side of the triangle.
9. There will now be a square in the middle of the triangle.

BASIC FOLD 2 (SQUARE FOLD)

1. With the right side facing UP, fold the paper across from corner to corner to make a triangle.
2. Unfold and make the same fold across to the other corner. Unfold.
3. With the colour side now facing DOWN, fold the paper in half and unfold.
4. Fold it in half the other way and unfold.
5. Push the sides towards the centre crease to make a square.
6. Keeping the double square flat, fold the right-hand side over to the left-hand side, and fold the left-hand arrowed point of the square towards the centre at the top.
7. Take the right-hand side back again.
8. You now have a square with a kite shape in the centre.

Green-and-blue teabag card

I used the basic triangular fold, with a slight variation, to make this card.

YOU WILL NEED

» White cardstock:
  24 cm x 15 cm
» 8 teabag squares in shades
  of blue and green
» Blue-green patterned paper
  for the triangles
» Dark blue organza ribbon with
  white dots: 30 cm
» 2 square rhinestones
» Double-sided tape
» Glue pen
» Glue dots
» Bone folder

Method

1. Fold the teabag squares, following steps 1–5 of basic fold 1 as set out on p. 104.
2. Keeping the double triangle flat, bring the right-hand side over to the left-hand side and fold the left-hand side of the triangle parallel to the centre fold.
3. Fold the right-hand side back again.
4. Bring the left-hand side to the right and fold the right-hand side parallel to the centre fold.
5. Fold the left-hand side back again.
6. Use the glue pen to apply glue to the underside of the flap and interlink it with the next teabag square.
7. Repeat this to interlink all the teabag squares.
8. Score the white cardstock and fold it in half along the scored line to make the card.
9. Cut the blue-green triangle to be pasted from one corner of the card to the next.
10. Attach a strip of double-sided tape to the edge of the triangle.
11. Paste it on the white greeting card.
12. Leave open a 4 cm strip. Cut a blue-green triangle to fit into the top right-hand corner of the white card.
13. Attach a strip of tape to the edge of the triangle and stick it on the card.
14. Paste the teabag design in the centre of the white strip and decorate both sides with a square rhinestone using a glue dot.

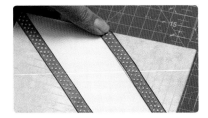

Windmill

This pink and white teabag card reminds me of a windmill. The folding is a variety of basic fold 1.

YOU WILL NEED

» 1 piece of purple cardstock: 28 cm x 14 cm
» 2 pieces of purple cardstock: 14 cm x 14 cm each
» Green dotted cardstock: 13 cm x 13 cm
» Light purple cardstock: 13 cm x 13 cm
» 8 pink and white teabag squares
» 7 white and/or light green buttons: different sizes
» Double-sided tape
» Glue dots
» Glue pen
» Pair of compasses of object with which to draw circles
» Bone folder

Method

1. Fold the teabag squares, following steps 1–5 of basic fold 1 as described on p. 104.
2. Open all the folds.
3. Fold the top two corners towards the centre of the square. The folds will already be there because of the earlier folding.
4. Press in the sides as indicated.
5. A square or diamond shape is visible on top of the triangle. This square stands out more than the one in basic fold 1 because it has actually been doubled.
6. Lift the square and fold the right-hand side of the triangle parallel to the centre fold.
7. Unfold the square.
8. Glue and paste the eight squares together to create a windmill shape.
9. On each of the pieces of purple 14 cm x 14 cm cardstock, draw a circle with a radius of 7 cm.
10. Draw a circle with a radius of 6,5 cm on the light purple as well as the green cardstock.

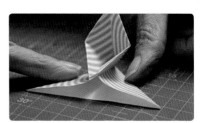

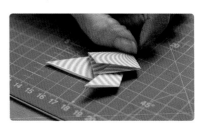

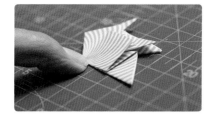

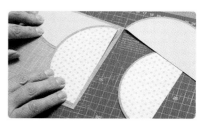

11. Cut out the circles and paste the green and light purple circles on the purple circle.
12. Cut the mounted circles exactly in half. You will have four circle halves.
13. Score and fold the big purple cardstock in half along the scored line to make the card.
14. Paste the four circle halves on the purple card, as the photograph illustrates.
15. Paste the teabag windmill exactly in the centre of the card.
16. Stick one large button in the centre of the windmill and arrange the other buttons as indicated.

To make this card, I used the basic triangular fold to make a rosette that will be pasted on the brim of the hat.

Yellow hat with rosette

YOU WILL NEED

» Yellow cardstock: A4 size
» Scarp piece of brown cardstock
» 8 teabag squares
» Gold pen
» Glue pen
» Double-sided tape

Method

1. Fold the eight teabag squares, following the instructions for basic fold 1 (p. 104).
2. Interlink the squares and use the glue pen to attach them.
3. Use the template on p. 193 to cut a hat of yellow cardstock. Fold as indicated.
4. Cut the band of the hat from the brown card-stock and attach it.
5. Use the gold pen to draw a line around the brim of the hat and the band.
6. Stick the teabag rosette onto the hat using double-sided tape.

Dashing contrast

The black-and-white patterned paper matched the black-and-white teabag paper so perfectly that I immediately wanted to put them together. This teabag design is a little more difficult than the other designs, but the method is set out clearly. The design is beautiful enough on both sides to be used as a Christmas decoration.

YOU WILL NEED

- » Black-and-white patterned paper
- » 8 black-and-white teabag squares
- » Silver glitter-glue
- » 1 round rhinestone: approximately 1,5 cm in diameter
- » Glue pen
- » Glue dots
- » Ruler
- » Bone folder

Method

1. Fold the teabag square, following steps 1–7 of basic fold 2 as indicated on p. 104.
2. Score the top of the kite shape, using a ruler and a bone folder to create a fold line.
3. Open the bottom end of the kite shape.
4. Flatten the sides.
5. Interlink the eight teabag squares and paste them together to make a star.
6. The back of the star is as beautiful and that is why this star can be used as a Christmas decoration.
7. Score and fold the black-and-white patterned paper in half along the scored line to make the card.
8. Stick the star in the corner of the card and use a glue dot to attach the round rhinestone.
9. Use the silver glitter-glue to decorate the card as you see fit.

Cheerful butterfly

Instead of the usual eight teabag squares, only two are used to create this butterfly card.

YOU WILL NEED

- » Cream-coloured pearlescent cardstock: 22 cm x 15 cm
- » 2 teabag squares in shades of brown and pink
- » Thin strips of paper in the same shades of brown and pink
- » Small piece of gold cardstock for the body
- » Flower craft punch
- » Scrap pieces of pink paper for the flowers
- » Glue pen
- » Gold pen
- » Ruler
- » Bone folder

Method

1. Fold the teabag squares in half diagonally, with the patterned side facing down.
2. Fold it in half again, without unfolding it.
3. Open the second fold.
4. Fold the top of the triangle until a quarter of it protrudes over the bottom edge.
5. Slant the right-hand side downwards towards the centre.
6. Repeat on the left-hand side.
7. Cut the body of the butterfly from a scrap piece of gold card.
8. Score and fold the cream-coloured pearlescent cardstock in half along the scored line to make the card.
9. Stick the body and wings of the butterfly on the card.
10. Use the gold pen to draw the antennae.
11. Stick strips of brown and pink paper approximately 1 cm from the base and right-hand side of the card.
12. Punch out four small pink paper flowers and paste them as indicated.

Threadfully creative

Two techniques that work well with thread are spirelli and prick and stitch. Both techniques look exceptional if you use metallic thread to make the card.

Red-and-green prick and stitch card

This card is made very quickly and, once you understand the pattern, it will be easy to make several cards at a time.

YOU WILL NEED

» White pearlescent cardstock: 29,5 cm x 10 cm
» Red and green metallic thread
» Thick pin
» Thin needle
» Polystyrene square or special pricking mat
» Ruler
» Bone folder
» Sticky tape

Method

1. Score the cardstock at 10 cm and 20 cm. Fold the panels over each other. The embroidery is done on the middle panel and one of the side panels will cover the reverse side of the embroidery.
2. Copy the template on p. 194 and stick it to the middle panel of the card temporarily.
3. Place the cardstock and template on the polystyrene square or pricking mat and make holes in the card with the pin.
4. Remove the template and hold the cardstock against the light to make sure that you have made all the holes.
5. Embroider all the red flowers first, following the pattern.
6. Embroider the green leaves, following the pattern.
7. Make sure that the thread is fixed securely on the reverse side. Do not be concerned about the neatness – this section will be covered.
8. Apply glue to the smaller side panel and stick it to the middle panel of the card.

Japanese spirelli card

This card contains a touch of Eastern enchantment and the gold and red colour combination contributes towards the warm feel.

YOU WILL NEED

- » White textured cardstock: 21 cm x 20 cm
- » 10 red circles 2 cm in diameter
- » 12 small red punched flowers
- » Black acrylic paint
- » Thin paintbrush
- » Craft knife or deckle-edged scissors
- » Gold glitter-glue
- » Gold metallic thread
- » Glue pen
- » Glue dots
- » Ruler
- » Bone folder

Method

1. Score and fold the white cardstock in half along the scored line to make the card.
2. Copy the tree template on p. 195.
3. Paint the tree black using the thin paintbrush and acrylic paint.
4. Cut 16 slits around the edges of each of the circles. You can use a craft knife or the serrated scissors. Fortunately, I have a punch that is exactly the right size and it has a notched edge.
5. Wind the gold thread around the red, notched circles as indicated. The thread is secured to the back of the circles with glue dots.
6. Use any small flower punch for the red flowers. I used the same punch that is used on p. 53. It is an edge punch.
7. Arrange and paste the circles and flowers as indicated. I used a glue pen for the small flowers and glue dots for the circles.
8. Apply a drop of gold glitter-glue to the centre of each of the small flowers.

Sparkling spirelli

The focal point of this card is the purple spirelli with the round rhinestone in the centre. I drew the card pattern with the 32 points on my computer, but I have included the template for you. It appears on p. 195. This card is also rather quick and easy to make.

YOU WILL NEED

- » Purple cardstock: 22 cm x 15 cm
- » Light purple cardstock: 14 cm x 10 cm
- » White cardstock for the spirelli pattern
- » Purple metallic thread
- » Round rhinestones: 3 large, 1 medium and 1 small
- » Dotted purple ribbon: 12 cm
- » Floral purple ribbon: 16 cm
- » Double-sided tape
- » Glue
- » Adhesive foam tape
- » Ruler
- » Bone folder

Method

1. Score and fold the purple cardstock in half along the scored line to make the card.
2. Copy the template for the spirelli on p. 195.
3. Wind the purple thread around the spirelli as follows:
   - Secure the thread at the back of the cardstock.
   - Start at the top notch and skip 12 notches. Follow the pattern as indicated on the template.
   - Repeat until the pattern is complete.
4. Stick the floral ribbon 1,5 cm from the base of the card. Fold it around the back of the card.
5. Stick the dotted ribbon 1 cm from the left-hand side of the card and fold it around the edges.
6. Now attach the light purple cardstock to the greeting card.
7. Use adhesive foam tape to attach the spirelli in the corner where the two ribbons meet. The foam tape will add dimension.
8. Attach the round rhinestones with glue dots as indicated.

Alcohol ink

As the name suggests, this ink has a very high alcohol content and, consequently, it dries very quickly. This makes it perfect for use on non-porous surfaces such as glossy cardstock, acetate, plastic or metal. You can even use it to dye buttons. The possibilities are endless and I would love to write a book about it some day!

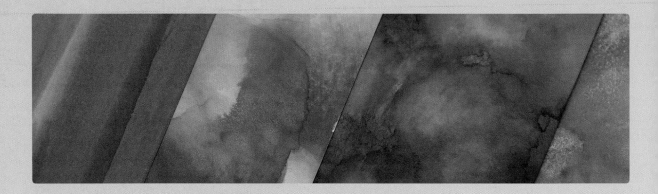

Basic technique for using alcohol ink

1. The ink is usually applied to the surface using an ink applicator. The applicator consists of a handle, which is attached to a wooden block that has Velcro pasted underneath it. You can attach felt squares to the Velcro and use it to apply the ink.
2. Drip two to three drops of the colour you have chosen onto the applicator. You can decide how many colours you want to use simultaneously. Two to three colours work well.
3. You can use various motions to create different effects with the ink on the applicator.
4. You can tap it or draw lines, or swirl the applicator around while pressing down on the cardstock.
5. You receive a blending solution with the alcohol ink. This allows the colours to flow into one another.
6. A copper-, silver- or pearl-coloured mix can be added to the colours.

In this example, I used three colours to draw lines on one of the cards while I simply pressed the ink onto the other card and twisted the applicator. One of the cards illustrates the effect created by adding the copper-coloured mix. Depending on your choice of colours, you can create the most beautiful surfaces for making cards.

Blue, purple and pink card

YOU WILL NEED

» Light-blue cardstock: 18 cm x 16 cm
» Purple cardstock: 15 cm x 8 cm
» White glossy cardstock: 14 cm x 7 cm
» 3 colours alcohol ink: for this specific card, I used Raspberry, Pool and Watermelon.
» Alcohol ink applicator
» Glue
» Ruler
» Bone folder

Method

1. Score and fold the blue cardstock in half along the scored line to make the card.
2. Stick the purple cardstock onto the blue, leaving a blue border around the purple.
3. Drip the alcohol ink onto the applicator as described under the basic technique on p. 124.
4. Press the applicator on the top two-thirds of the glossy paper and draw lines on the lower third.
5. Stick the glossy cardstock onto the purple cardstock.

To make this card, I combined two of the techniques described on p. 124. The top half of the card was created by pressing the ink onto the cardstock; on the lower half I drew lines. What makes this technique so interesting is the fact that you will never get exactly the same effect twice.

Hint: I always use a whole A5 size cardstock for the inking and then choose the section to use for the card. The off-cuts can be used on smaller cards or as labels.

Card with plastic plaques

Plastic embellishments are available in a variety of shapes and sizes. You are most likely to find them in scrapbook shops. To make this card, I first used alcohol ink to decorate the plastic plaques before stamping motifs onto them.

YOU WILL NEED

- » Dark pink cardstock: 28 cm x 14 cm
- » Dark purple velvet cardstock: 13 cm x 13 cm
- » Light pink pearlescent cardstock: 12 cm x 12 cm
- » 3 square plastic plaques: 3 cm x 3 cm each
- » Flower craft stamp
- » Inkpad: black
- » Pink, blue and purple alcohol ink
- » Alcohol ink applicator
- » Glue
- » Glue dots
- » Ruler
- » Bone folder

Method

1. Score and fold the dark pink cardstock in half along the scored line to create the card.
2. Stick the dark purple velvet paper and the light pink pearlescent paper onto the card using the matting technique (p. 15).
3. Pour the three alcohol ink colours onto the applicator and press it onto the plastic discs.
4. Allow the paint to dry and then stamp the flower motifs in black ink onto the reverse side of the plaques. (The ink and stamp must not be on the same side.)
5. Stick the plaques onto the card diagonally from left to right using glue dots.

Glass paint for cards

Using glass paint to create cards is like painting a little picture for someone. Glass paint does not have to be used only on glass – it works well on all non-porous surfaces. It looks beautiful on metal surfaces, and for card-making it can be used on acetate and plastic. There are two types, namely water-based and solvent-based glass paints. Water-based glass paint is ideal for children to use, because they can simply wash their hands, and the paintbrushes, in water. Solvent-based glass paint can only be removed with acetone, but the colours are intense and bright. For the cards in this book, I have used the latter.

Cheerful butterfly

I used grey liquid lead instead of black to create this butterfly because I wanted to give it a gentler look. The light glass-paint colours are the result of adding large amounts of colourless glass paint to the dark colours. Do not use white paint to lighten the colours, as this would rob them of their translucency and leave them opaque.

YOU WILL NEED

- » Pink cardstock: 28 cm × 14 cm
- » White pearlescent cardstock: 13,3 cm × 13,5 cm
- » Acetate: 13,3 cm × 13,5 cm
- » Grey liquid lead (liquid liner)
- » Glass paint: colourless, purple, yellow, red and brown
- » Silver sticky tape
- » Double-sided tape
- » Glue dots
- » Craft knife
- » Ruler
- » Bone folder

Method

1. Copy the pattern on p. 196 and trace the pattern on the acetate using grey liquid lead.
2. Follow steps 1–5 as set out on p. 131–132 for the African face. To obtain the light glass-paint colours, you have to start with colourless paint and add the bright colours until you are satisfied with the mix.
3. Stick silver sticky tape around the edges of the acetate. It is not only decorative, but it also strengthens the acetate.
4. Use the craft knife to cut the wings of the butterfly away from the liquid lead outline. Cut only up to the body of the butterfly.
5. Place glue dots on the body of the butterfly and paste it onto the white pearlescent card.
6. Score and fold the pink cardstock in half along the scored line to make the card.
7. Paste the white cardstock with the glass-painted butterfly onto the pink card.
8. Curve the cut wings slight upwards so that they stand out a little.

Multi-coloured African face

The African face lends itself to beautiful, bright colours, and in a black frame it might as well decorate a wall as a work of art. You can change the colours as you wish, but the bright, strong primary colours work best for this design.

YOU WILL NEED

- » Black cardstock: A4 size
- » Black glossy cardstock: A5 size
- » Acetate: A5 size
- » Felt-tip pen
- » Black liquid lead (liquid liner)
- » Glass paint: red, orange, brown, blue, green, purple and yellow
- » Acetone
- » Aluminium foil: slightly larger than A5
- » Double-sided tape
- » Craft knife
- » Ruler
- » Bone folder

Method

1. Copy the template on p. 195 and trace it on the acetate with a felt-tip pen.
2. Turn the acetate over and go over the lines again using the liquid lead.
3. Always work from top to bottom when you are using liquid lead, to prevent your hand or sleeve from accidentally smudging the lines. Complete the entire design and make sure that the liquid lead is completely dry before moving on to the next step.
4. Once the liquid lead has dried, it will take on a matt finish. That is when you can start applying the glass paint. Use a paintbrush and load the paint on it from the bottle.

5. Finish all the sections of the same colour before moving to a new colour. Be sure to clean your brushes thoroughly in acetone before you start applying a new colour. Finish painting all the sections as indicated on the diagram. Leave the design in a dust-free area until it has dried completely. If you are pressed for time, use a hair-dryer to dry the paint.
6. Crinkle the aluminium foil carefully.
7. Unfold it carefully. DO NOT roll the foil into a tight ball – you will not be able to unfold it.
8. Cut the foil to the size of the acetate and paste it onto the side which you have painted, using double-sided tape.
9. Use a craft knife to cut a 13 cm x 9 cm window in the A5 glossy cardstock. (It must be 3 cm from the left- and right-hand sides, and 4 cm from the top and base.)
10. Stick the acetate and foil to the reverse side of the window with double-sided tape.
11. Score and fold the black A4 cardstock in half along the scored line to make the card.
12. Stick the glass design in the A5 frame onto the front of the card.

Red-cheeked sun

If you wish to use glass paint in delicate designs, working with liquid lead can be difficult. An alternative would be to use tracing paper and then apply the glass paint with a toothpick.

YOU WILL NEED

» Cream-coloured pearlescent cardstock: 22 cm x 11 cm
» Orange cardstock: 10,5 cm x 10,5 cm
» Acetate: 10 cm x 10 cm
» Craft knife
» Tracing paper
» Double-sided tape
» Glass paint: orange and yellow
» Paintbrush
» Ruler
» Bone folder

Method

1. Carefully stick the sun sticker onto the acetate.
2. Paint the sun's cheeks on the front with orange glass paint.
3. Wait until the orange paint has dried completely and then paint the background yellow.
4. Score and fold the cream-coloured cardstock in half along the scored line to make the card.
5. Use the craft knife to cut a 8,5 cm x 8,5 cm window in the front of the card.
6. Stick the acetate onto the inside of the window with double-sided tape.
7. Cut a window from the orange card to leave a 1 cm border.
8. Stick the orange border onto the front of the card, over the window.

Sunny sunflowers

If you wish to use glass paint in delicate designs, working with liquid lead can be difficult. An alternative would be to use tracing paper and then apply the glass paint with a toothpick.

YOU WILL NEED

» Bright yellow cardstock:
  14 cm × 8 cm
» Acetate: 6 cm × 6 cm
» Tracing paper
» Glass paint: green, yellow
  and red
» 4 toothpicks
» Craft knife
» Double-sided tape
» Ruler
» Bone folder

Method

1. Carefully remove the sticker from the sheet and paste it onto the acetate.
2. Fill the spaces with glass paint. Use a toothpick to apply the paint and work on the side on which the sticker has been pasted.
3. Score and fold the yellow cardstock in half along the scored line to make the card.
4. Use the craft knife to cut a 5 cm x 6 cm window in the front of the card. (It must extend 1 cm from all the sides.)
5. Stick the acetate to the inside of the window with double-sided tape.

Appealing embellishments

Embellishments make the work of many a card maker and scrapbook enthusiast so much easier! A seemingly endless range – it is impossible to mention everything – is readily available. In this chapter, the emphasis is on metal shapes (embellishment charms), handmade stickers and paper flowers.

METAL EMBELLISHMENT SHAPES

These cute metal shapes are ideal for Father's Day or Mother's Day cards. The same technique can be used for both cards.

Tool card

YOU WILL NEED

» Light brown cardstock: 26 cm x 14 cm
» Blue cardstock: 13,5 cm x 12,5 cm
» Patterned paper: 13,5 cm x 12,5 cm
» Metal shapes: tools
» Craft knife
» Glue dots
» Double-sided tape
» Ruler
» Bone folder

Method

1. Score and fold the light brown cardstock in half along the scored line to make the card.
2. Use double-sided tape to stick the patterned paper on the front of the card.
3. Cut three windows in the blue cardstock: two of 5 cm x 5 cm each, and one of 10,5 cm x 6 cm.
4. Use double-sided tape to mount this on the patterned paper and card.
5. Use glue dots to paste the metal shapes in the blue frames on the patterned paper.

Needlework themed card

YOU WILL NEED

» Light brown cardstock: 26 cm x 14 cm
» Brown-and-pink striped paper:
   13,5 x 12,5 cm
» Patterned paper: 13,5 cm x 12,5 cm
» Metal shapes: needlework theme
» Craft knife
» Glue dots
» Double-sided tape
» Ruler
» Bone folder

Method

1. Score and fold the light brown cardstock in half along the scored line to make the card.
2. Paste the patterned paper on the front of the card using double-sided tape.
3. Cut a window in the striped paper to create a 1 cm border around the sides of the card.
4. Use double-sided tape to mount the border on the patterned paper.
5. Use glue dots to stick the shapes in position.

PAPER FLOWERS

Paper flowers are available in various shapes, sizes and colours. You can even colour flowers that have not been dyed yourself. You can use colour pens, inkpads, glitter glue or ordinary colour crayons to colour the flowers. If you combine these methods, you can create the most interesting cards.

Stylish simplicity

YOU WILL NEED

- » Cream-coloured pearlescent cardstock: 22 cm x 15 cm
- » 9 natural paper flowers: various sizes
- » 16 paste-on pearls
- » 4 laser-cut corners
- » Glue dots
- » Glue pen
- » Ruler
- » Bone folder

Method

1. Score and fold the cream-coloured pearlescent cardstock in half along the scored line to make the card.
2. Use various combinations of the paper flowers and stick them on the front of the card with glue dots.
3. Use the glue pen to paste the pearls and the wooden corners.

Black and white flowers

A combination of black and white always looks stunning and stylish. Simply change the combinations and accessories that are used with the flowers to create a unique card.

Left-hand card

YOU WILL NEED

» Black cardstock: 18 cm x 13 cm
» Cuttlebug™
» Silver paper: 10 cm x 7 cm
» 2 paper flowers: 1 black and 1 white
» 1 small, round rhinestone
» 1 black, round split pin
» 1 transparency with design
» Glue wheel
» Glue dots
» Glue pen
» Ruler
» Bone folder

Method

1. Score and fold the black cardstock in half along the scored line to make the card.
2. Emboss the front of the card using the Cuttlebug™.
3. Paste the transparency on the silver paper and mount it on the front of the card.
4. Stick the two flowers together using a glue dot, and glue them to the transparency.
5. Use the glue pen to paste the rhinestones in the middle of the flowers.
6. Push the split pin through the left-hand corner of the silver paper and the card and open it.

Right-hand card

YOU WILL NEED

» Black cardstock: 22 cm x 17 cm
» Grey patterned paper: 15 cm x 10 cm
» 3 pieces of satin ribbon (black, grey and white): each 7 mm wide and 17 cm long
» 6 black and white paper flowers: various sizes
» 3 round rhinestones
» 3 floral stones
» 1 black, round split pin
» Double-sided tape
» Glue pen
» Glue dots
» Ruler
» Bone folder

Method

1. Score and fold the black cardstock in half along the scored line to make the card.
2. Use the double-sided tape to stick the ribbons onto the grey patterned paper, 2 cm apart.
3. Use various combinations of the paper flowers and stick them on the paper using glue dots.
4. Use the glue pen to attach the rhinestones to the ribbon.
5. Glue the patterned paper to the front of the card.
6. Push the split pin through the largest flower and fold the pin on the inside of the card.

HANDMADE STICKERS

Handmade stickers are very popular, because one sheet usually contains more than one sticker and these can be used on several cards or scrapbook pages. They are not cheap, but it is still cheaper to buy handmade stickers and make your own cards than to buy cards. The greatest advantage of the handmade stickers is that you basically only need cardstock to create a lovely product.

Beach scene

YOU WILL NEED

» White cardstock: 15 cm x 9 cm
» Stickers
» Ruler
» Bone folder

Method

1. Score and fold the white cardstock in half along the scored line to make the card.
2. The stickers already have glue squares on the reverse side. Peel off the backing paper and paste the stickers on the card.

Round boxes

YOU WILL NEED

» Pink cardstock: 12 cm x 8 cm
» Gold-coloured cardstock: 7 cm x 5 cm
» Glue wheel
» Handmade sticker
» Ruler
» Bone folder

Method

1. Score and fold the pink cardstock in half along the scored line to make the card.
2. Use the glue wheel to paste the gold card on the greeting card.
3. Peel off the backing paper and stick the design on the card.

Bright pink with black lace

Even though this card is made using a bought sticker, I have provided a template for the dress (see p. 197). You can use scrap bits of material and lace to design your own dress. Ribbon roses, like the ones on the dress, are readily available at needlework and scrapbook outlets.

YOU WILL NEED

» White pearlescent cardstock: 16 cm x 12 cm
» Printed transparency
» Handmade dress sticker
» Glue dots
» Ruler
» Bone folder

Method

1. Score and fold the white cardstock in half along the scored line to make the card.
2. Paste the transparency on the card using glue dots.
3. Peel off the backing tape and paste the sticker on the transparency.

From the sewing basket

HAVE FUN WITH FELT AND BUTTONS

Because felt does not fray and is available in so many colours, it is the ideal material to use for card making. The possibilities are truly endless and you can give your imagination and creativity free rein. You can make the most beautiful cards with buttons, because the available range is extensive; and beads that are pasted on felt always look stunning too.

Flowers using mother-of-pearl buttons

The mother-of-pearl buttons look soft on the green pearlescent cardstock and they match the embossed background beautifully.

YOU WILL NEED

» Soft green pearlescent paper:
  21 cm x 13 cm
» 21 mother-of-pearl buttons:
  3 colours and various sizes
» Cuttlebug™
» Glue dots
» Ruler
» Bone folder

Method

1. Score and fold the green cardstock in half along the scored line to make the card.
2. Emboss the front of the card using the Cuttlebug™.
3. Use glue dots to stick the buttons on the card. Arrange them in groups of seven to resemble flowers.

Cute cupcakes

Using beads, felt and glitter glue, you can create the most incredible cupcakes. You can change the colours of the cupcakes, or use other beads than the ones I have used in the example. It is not necessary to buy the exact materials used in the examples. Scratch around in your cupboards and use what you have available.

YOU WILL NEED

» Pink cardstock: 29 cm x 10 cm
» Patterned paper that matches the cardstock: 14 cm x 9 cm
» Felt: brown, pink, light pink and white
» A few pink seed beads
» A pair of sharp fabric scissors
» Gold glitter glue
» Toothpick
» Glue wheel
» Craft glue
» Adhesive foam tape
» Bone folder

Method

1. Score and fold the pink cardstock in half along the scored line to make the card.
2. Use the glue wheel to paste the patterned paper onto the card.
3. Copy the cupcake template on p. 196 and cut it out as indicated.
4. Use the glitter glue to draw four gold lines on the baking base of the cupcake and allow the glue to dry.
5. Spread craft glue on the bright pink section and paste it on the baking base.
6. Stick the white section on top of the bright pink felt.
7. Dot craft glue on the white felt and place the seed beads on the glue dots.
8. Use the toothpick to pick up the beads and paste them on the felt.
9. Paste a small pink circle on top of the cupcake.
10. Make a smaller cupcake, using the same method.
11. Attach adhesive foam tape to the reverse side of the cupcake; use a double layer for the larger cupcake.
12. Stick the cupcakes into position on the card.

In full bloom

The black card provides a beautiful contrast for the bright colours of the buttons and felt. Remember to paste light-coloured paper inside a black card to make writing the message easier. If you are going to be using the card yourself, you could use any light milky pen for the message.

YOU WILL NEED

» Black cardstock: A4 size
» 4 buttons: 2 large, bright ones and 2 smaller floral ones
» Orange and green felt
» Striped ribbon: 40 cm long and 1 cm wide
» Bright pink and green embroidery thread
» Embroidery needle
» A pair of sharp fabric scissors
» Double-sided tape
» Glue dots
» Ruler
» Bone folder

Method

1. Score and fold the black cardstock in half along the scored line to make the card.
2. Use the template on p. 197 and cut out two orange and two green felt flowers.
3. Using blanket stitch, sew the two flowers of the same colour together.
4. Sew a large, brightly coloured and a small, floral button onto the centre of each felt flower.
5. Use double-sided tape to stick the ribbon 2 cm from the left-hand side and 2,5 cm from the base of the card.
6. Position and paste the two felt flowers as shown using glue dots.

Felt butterfly

YOU WILL NEED

» Purple cardstock: 23 cm x 11,5 cm
» Yellow felt square: 9 cm x 9 cm
» Purple and green felt for the butterfly
» 1 large purple button
» A pair of sharp fabric scissors
» Gold sticky tape
» Glue dots
» Double-sided tape
» Ruler
» Bone folder

Method

1. Score the purple cardstock 11 cm from the left-hand side and fold it along the scored line. Once folded, the one side of the card will be approximately 5 mm longer than the other side.
2. Stick the ribbon onto the longer side.
3. Use the template on p. 197 and cut out a purple and a green felt butterfly as shown.
4. Sew the purple and green felt together with a button in the centre.
5. Use double-sided tape to stick the yellow felt square onto the card.
6. Use glue dots to stick the butterfly on the yellow felt.

Black and white stripes – with buttons and felt

Originally, the black and silver felt wheels were used for making jewellery, but they look beautiful in combination with the buttons on this card. It is quick and easy to make the felt wheels and they will look as pretty in bright colours.

YOU WILL NEED

- » White cardstock: 20 cm x 20 cm
- » Silver ribbon: 36 cm long and 7 mm wide
- » Black felt strip: 42 cm x 7 cm
- » Square craft punch
- » Black-and-white patterned paper
- » 2 black-and-white buttons
- » Needle and black thread
- » Glue dots
- » Glue pen
- » Ruler
- » Bone folder

Method

1. Cut the ribbon and the black felt strip into three equal parts. The ribbon must be 12 cm long, and the black felt 14 cm.
2. Place the ribbon on the black felt and roll them up together into a tight ball.
3. Sew the end of the wheel in place using top-sewing stitch.
4. Score and fold the white cardstock in half along the scored line to make the card.
5. Punch five squares proportionally along the long, open end of the card.
6. Decorate the edges of the squares, as well as the inside edge of the card, using small frames of black-and-white patterned paper. Use the glue pen because you are working with thin strips of paper.
7. Stick the felt wheels and buttons alternately on the inside of the card, opposite the punched squares.

Colourful felt wheels

You can change the colours of this card to suit you. It will also look stunning if you use various shades of the same colour, for example shades of pink or blue, etc. Another possibility is to combine one colour with black.

YOU WILL NEED

» Bright yellow cardstock: 22 cm x 13 cm
» Black felt rectangle: 11 cm x 10 cm
» 7 small yellow and white buttons
» Felt for 7–8 circles of different colours
» Embroidery thread and needle
» A pair of sharp fabric scissors
» Glue dots
» Double-sided tape

Method

1. Score and fold the bright yellow cardstock in half along the scored line to make the card.
2. Use double-sided tape to stick the black rectangle onto the card.
3. Cut seven circles, 2,5 cm in diameter, from the various colours of felt.
4. Cut another seven smaller circles, approximately 1,5 cm in diameter.
5. Stitch a small and a large circle and a button together using the embroidery thread and needle.
6. Vary the colours so that the colour combinations of the felt circles are all different.
7. Use glue dots to stick the circles that have been sewn together randomly onto the black felt.

More felt wheels

YOU WILL NEED

- » Brown cardstock: 23 cm x 20 cm
- » Brown-and-pink patterned paper
- » Silver patterned paper: 23 cm x 2 cm
- » Silver cardstock: 9 cm x 6,5 cm
- » Transparency with printed design: 9 cm x 6,5 cm
- » Black cardstock: 10 cm x 8 cm
- » 3 felt wheels: made as described on p. 159
- » 5 round rhinestones: 4 crystal, 1 pink
- » White organza ribbon: 50 cm long and 5 mm wide
- » A pair of deckle-edged scissors
- » Glue dots
- » Glue wheel
- » Glue pen
- » Ruler and bone folder

Method

1. Score and fold the brown cardstock in half along the scored line to make the card. Please note that it is a long, narrow card.
2. Paste the silver patterned paper onto the long, open end of the brown card, leaving approximately 5 mm to stick over the edge of the card.
3. Use the deckle-edged scissors to trim the protruding edge.
4. Paste the brown-and-pink patterned paper onto the front of the card.
5. Cut a wavy edge on the black cardstock.
6. Stick the black cardstock, silver cardstock and transparency together and paste it on the card as indicated.
7. Use glue dots to stick the felt wheels onto the card, and use the glue pen to attach the rhinestones.
8. Tie the ribbon in the card fold and make a bow on the outside.

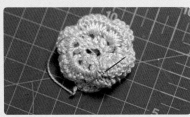

Crocheted flower card

When I attended a Women's Association meeting one morning, I received this very interesting crochet flower pattern. The flower is made by crocheting one long "worm" and then winding it around and around to make the three-layered flower. The flower looks beautiful on a card; because thread is used for the crocheting, it is not too bulky.

YOU WILL NEED

» Cream-coloured pearlescent cardstock: 15 cm x 11,5 cm
» Brown pearlescent cardstock: 10,5 cm x 7 cm
» DMC crochet thread no. 8 in Ecru
» Crochet hook no. 2.5
» Brown 6 mm glass pearl
» Cuttlebug™
» Glue wheel
» Glue dot
» Ruler
» Bone folder

Method

Crochet flower pattern:
Abbreviations: dc = double crochet; tc = treble crochet; ch = chain stitch

1. Start with 35 chain stitches.
2. 1st row: tc in the 5th ch from the hook. *1 dc, skip 1 ch (1 tc 1 dc 1 tc) in the next ch.* Repeat from * to * to end. You will have 16 V-shaped groups of stitches.
3. 2nd row: 3 ch = 1 tc, 5 tc in the 1st ch space, *dc in next ch space, 6 tc in next space.* Repeat from * to * to end. End with 6 tc in the last ch space. The flower "worm" will resemble the illustration.
4. Roll up the flower, starting at the inside, and sew the reverse side as indicated.

To make the rest of the card:

1. Score and fold the cream-coloured cardstock in half along the scored line to make the card.
2. Emboss and cut the round border pattern using the Cuttlebug™.
3. Paste the brown border pattern onto the cream-coloured card.
4. Use a glue dot to stick the crocheted flower on the card and paste the pearl in the centre of the flower.

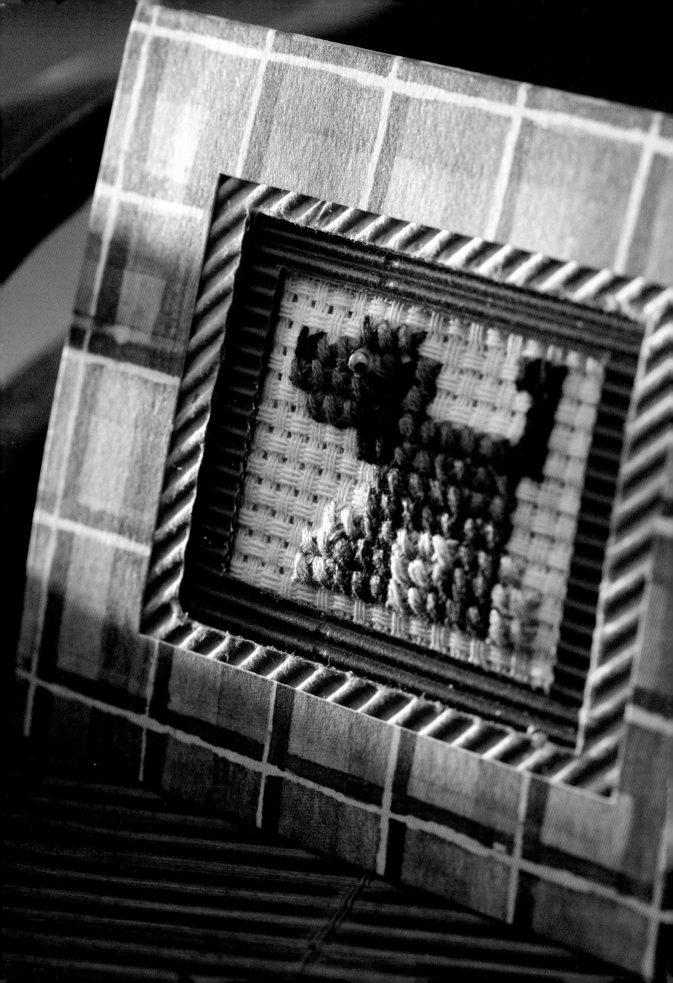

Ever-popular cross-stitch

Cross-stitching is one of my passions, and it is extremely satisfying to embroider a small design to use on a card. In my book *Cross-stitch miniatures* you will find more than 80 designs, comprising approximately 50 x 50 stitches, which are ideally suited for use on cards. I have included four of these patterns here.

MOUNTING OF CROSS-STITCH CARDS

When you use cross-stitching to make a card, you have to prepare a card with a window or opening and three panels. The design is visible through the window or opening and one of the panels covers the reverse side of the cross-stitch work. When you mount the embroidered work, make sure that it is securely attached around the opening. Go the extra mile with the mounting so that you handiwork will be displayed at its best.

Method

1. Determine the size of your embroidery and cut the cardstock so that it is at least three times as wide as the design. I also add 1 cm to each side of the design.
2. The height of the cardstock is also determined by the size of the design. Be careful not to use too small a piece of cardstock.
3. Divide the cardstock into three equal parts and score and fold the cardstock along the scored lines.
4. Use a craft knife to cut the opening in the centre of the middle panel of your greeting card.
5. Apply double-sided tape right around the opening, as closely as possible to the edge of the opening.
6. Peel off the backing tape and stick the embroidered design to it. Make sure that it is dead centre.
7. Apply double-sided tape to the panel that is to cover the design.
8. Peel off the backing tape of the double-sided tape and secure the panel firmly to the reverse side of the design.

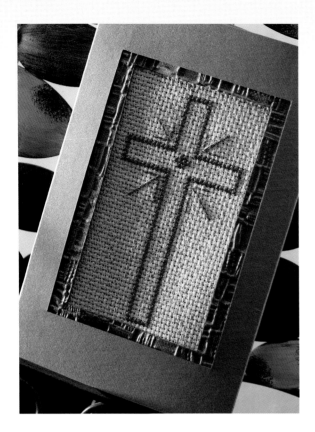

This card is quick and easy to make, because you only stitch the straight sections. You can definitely finish it in one evening. Make the mounting really special by adding a contrasting colour as a border around the design.

Classical cross

YOU WILL NEED

» Dark green pearlescent cardstock: 30 cm x 16 cm
» Bronze patterned paper: 13 cm x 9,5 cm
» Corn-coloured 14-count Aida embroidery fabric: 25 cm x 15 cm
» Embroidery thread as pattern specifies
» Blunt-nosed embroidery needle
» Double-sided tape
» Craft knife
» Ruler
» Bone folder

Method

1. Embroider the cross according to the design (p. 198). Use two threads for the cross-stitching and one for the backstitching.
2. Score and fold the gold-coloured cardstock along the scored lines at 10 cm and 20 cm to make three panels.
3. Cut a 11,5 cm x 7,5 cm window in the middle panel.
4. Cut a 10,5 cm x 6 cm window in the bronze patterned paper.
5. Paste the bronze patterned paper on the inside of the front panel using double-sided tape.
6. Attach the embroidered design as indicated on p. 166.

For Christmas

YOU WILL NEED

» Red cardstock for the snowman:
  30 cm x 10,5 cm
» Red cardstock for the candy stick:
  24 cm x 10 cm
» White 14-count even-weave linen for each
  design: 10 cm x 10 cm
» Embroidery thread as pattern specifies
» Blunt-nosed embroidery needle
» Double-sided tape
» Ruler
» Bone folder

Method

1. Embroider the motifs according to the designs
   (p. 199).
2. Use two threads for the cross-stitching and
   one for the backstitching.
3. Mount the motifs as indicated on p. 166.

The designs that I use for the cards are also suitable decorations to adorn a Christmas tree or an Advent calendar.

Even though these designs are not as simple as the cross, they can still be completed in a jiffy. The snowman is mounted on cardstock that is slightly larger than that used for the candy stick.

Use metallic thread for that extra special Christmas finish.

Cute doggy

YOU WILL NEED

» Green-and-brown patterned cardstock:
  26 cm x 12 cm
» Light brown corrugated paper:
  9 cm x 7 cm (cut a 6,5 cm x 4,5 cm window)
» Dark brown corrugated paper:
  9 cm x 7 cm (cut a 5 cm x 3,5 cm window)
» 8-count Aida embroidery fabric: 5 cm x 5 cm
» Embroidery thread as pattern specifies
» Blunt-nosed embroidery needle
» 1 paste-on googly eye
» Craft glue
» Double-sided tape
» Craft knife
» Ruler
» Bone folder

Method

1. Embroider the dog according to the design
   (p. 198).
2. Use six threads for the cross-stitching.
3. Glue on the eye with craft glue.
4. Mount according to the photograph, and refer
   to the steps on p. 166.

This pattern is so easy, a child will be able to stitch it. The motif is embroidered on 8-count Aida embroidery fabric, which means that the crosses are nice and big and children will easily master the skill. I once found the cute green frame in a magazine and only adapted it slightly to match the doggy motif.

Edible cards

The latest cute craze is to give someone an edible card on a special occasion – a message written on a biscuit.

The cards in this chapter are made according to a simple biscuit recipe and all the embellishments are made of plastic (fondant) icing. These are attached to the biscuit using royal icing as "glue". It is hard work making the plastic icing – that is why I usually buy it instead. All I then need to do is to add food-colouring to create different colours. Bake enough cakes for everyone at home to enjoy!

To "write" the message, mix the icing sugar and water and use baking paper to shape a piping bag.

BISCUIT RECIPE

INGREDIENTS

- » 80 g butter or margarine
- » 1¼ cup brown sugar
- » 1 egg
- » 100 ml golden syrup
- » 2 cups cake flour (and extra for rolling out)
- » ½ teaspoon ginger powder
- » ½ teaspoon cinnamon
- » 1 teaspoon baking soda

Method

1. Mix the butter or margarine, sugar, egg, golden syrup and water well.
2. Add all the dry ingredients and knead together until it forms a soft dough.
3. Sprinkle flour on the work surface and roll out the dough until it is about 5–7 mm thick.
4. Cut out the shapes using your favourite cutter.
5. Bake at 170 °C for 12 minutes (10 minutes if the biscuits are smaller).
6. It is a good idea to leave the biscuits in the warming oven for a while before you decorate them.

ROYAL ICING RECIPE

INGREDIENTS

- » 1 egg white
- » 1⅓ cup icing sugar
- » 1 teaspoon lemon juice
- » Colouring

Method

1. Mix all the ingredients using an electric mixer.
2. For the writing on the biscuits and detailed icing, you can make your own piping bag. Use baking paper rather than ordinary wax paper, since it is thicker.

PIPING BAG

1. Cut strong baking paper into a square of approximately 22 cm x 22 cm. Cut it diagonally to form two triangles. Each triangle makes a piping bag.
2. Keep the longest side of the triangle (AB) in a vertical position. Grip the centre of the side between the thumb and index finger of your right hand (at point T).
3. Use your left hand to move point A to point C to shape a cone.
4. Keep points A and C together and fold point B up to point A and C.
5. Fold points A, B and C together towards the inside of the cone.
6. Make a very small incision in the end of the cone through which the icing is pressed.

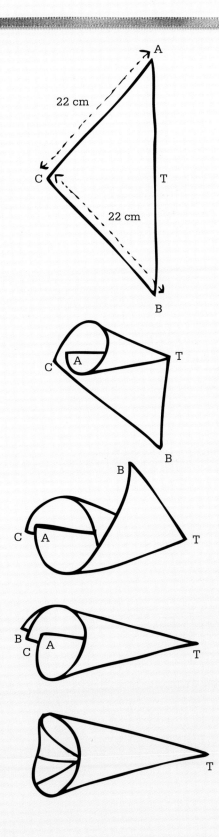

Merry Christmas

At Christmastime you can make several of these biscuits to serve to your guests. The round biscuits would look lovely on the Christmas tree and could be eaten on Christmas Day.

YOU WILL NEED

» Heart-shaped biscuit: approximately 10 cm high
» Plastic icing: red, light pink and white
» Royal icing
» Rolling pin
» Icing for writing: white and black

Method

1. Roll out the light pink, plastic icing and use a cookie cutter to cut a heart the same size as the biscuit.
2. Use the royal icing to fix it to the biscuit.
3. Roll out the red icing and cut another heart shape. Cut off approximately two thirds of the pointed end of the heart and stick it onto the light pink icing.
4. Roll out the white icing and use the cookie cutter to cut only the top of the heart to shape Santa's moustache.
5. Use the piping bag to make the brim of the hat.
6. Roll the white icing into a ball for the hat's tassel, and roll a light pink ball for Santa's nose. Make two small dots for the eyes.
7. Use the piping bag to write the message on the hat.

Merry Christmas

YOU WILL NEED

» Large, round biscuits: approximately 10 cm in diameter (make a hole on top of each before you bake them).
» White plastic icing
» Embossing template (I used one of the embossing folders from the Cuttlebug™).
» Royal icing
» Light blue plastic icing to write the message
» Rolling pin
» Light blue ribbon

Method

1. Roll out the white plastic icing and press it onto the embossed surface.
2. Cut it to the size of the biscuit and make a hole in it using a metal cookie cutter.
3. Stick it onto the biscuit using royal icing.
4. Use the light blue icing to write the message.
5. Thread the blue ribbon through the hole in the biscuit and hang it on the Christmas tree or on other Christmas decorations.

For my valentine

YOU WILL NEED

» 2 heart-shaped biscuits: approximately 10 cm high and 3 cm high
» Plastic icing: red and light pink
» Rolling pin
» Metal alphabet cookie cutters
» Royal icing

Method

1. Roll out the plastic icing and cut out a large light pink heart and a small red heart. Also use the cookie cutter to cut an "I" and a "U" from the red icing.
2. Stick the decoration onto the biscuits using royal icing.
3. Paste the small red heart on the big, light pink one and stick the "I" and "U" to the left and right of the heart.

Boy or girl?

To congratulate the mother of a new baby, give her an edible card. It will serve as an energy booster as well.

Baby boy

YOU WILL NEED

» Rectangular biscuit
» Plastic icing: light blue, bright blue and white
» Royal icing
» Rolling pin
» Alphabet cookie cutters
» Teddy bear cookie cutter

Method

1. Roll out the plastic icing and cut out the letters you need.
2. Cut the teddy bear from the light blue icing and cut two small circles from the white icing – one for the teddy bear's tummy and one for the nose.
3. Use royal icing and paste the shape onto the biscuit as indicated.
4. Use a piping bag to make small black eyes and a mouth for the bear.

Baby girl

YOU WILL NEED

» Rectangular biscuit
» Plastic icing: light pink, bright pink and white
» Royal icing
» Rolling pin
» Alphabet cookie cutters
» Pram cookie cutter

Method

1. Roll out the plastic icing and cut out the letters you need. Cut the pram from the bright pink icing, and cut two circles from the light pink icing to use as wheels for the pram.
2. Use royal icing and stick the shape onto the biscuit as indicated.
3. Use a piping bag to draw spokes on the wheels and folds on the pram cover.

Happy Easter

You can give this cute edible card, with a basket full of Easter eggs, to someone to celebrate Easter.

YOU WILL NEED

» Rectangular biscuit
» 2 rabbit-shaped biscuits
» Rolling pin
» Oval cookie cutter
» Bunny-shaped cookie cutter
» Small flower-shaped cookie cutter
» Plastic icing: green, pink, red, orange, blue, white, purple and yellow
» Royal icing

Method

1. Roll out the green icing and paste in on the rectangular biscuit with royal icing.
2. Follow the diagrams below to make the Easter eggs:

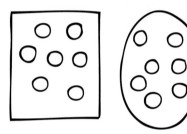

Red and purple egg:

» Use purple icing as background.
» Roll small red icing balls and place them on the purple background.
» Press down lightly on the balls with the rolling pin to flatten them and then cut out the egg using the oval cookie cutter.

Easter egg with stripes:

» You can use any colour as background.
» Roll the icing into little snakes using different colours and place them on the background.
» Roll lightly over the snakes with the rolling pin and cut out the egg using the oval cookie cutter.
» Stick the Easter eggs onto the green design.

3. Decorate the rest of the biscuit using the flowers and grass as indicated.
4. Use the piping bag to write a message in white on the biscuit.
5. Put the biscuit in a basket on a bit of hay, and add the two decorated bunnies and a few chocolate Easter eggs.

Say "thank you" the truly South African way

YOU WILL NEED

» Rectangular biscuit
» Plastic icing: light brown, dark brown and white
» Royal icing
» Rolling pin

Method

1. Roll out the icing and cut out a hut as indicated.
2. Use royal icing to stick the hut onto the biscuit.
3. Use the piping bag to write the message on the biscuit.

Welcome to South Africa!

YOU WILL NEED

» Rectangular biscuit
» Plastic icing: black, white, yellow, green, blue and red
» Royal icing
» Rolling pin

Method

1. Use white icing as background and roll it out to the same size as the biscuit.
2. Use the colours of the national flag, and cut the shapes from the various colours.
3. Place the colours in their proper places and roll lightly over them with the rolling pin.
4. Cut the flag to the size of the biscuit and stick it onto the biscuit with royal icing.
5. Use a piping bag to write the message on the biscuit.

Congratulate someone on an exceptional achievement by giving them this edible card!

You are a star!

YOU WILL NEED

» 1 large and 1 small star-shaped biscuit
» Plastic icing: orange and yellow
» Royal icing
» Large and small star cookie cutters
» Rolling pin

Method

1. Roll out the icing and cut a large star from the yellow icing and a small one from the orange icing.
2. Paste the shapes on the biscuits and stick the small star on the big one using royal icing.
3. Use the piping bag to write the message on the big star.
4. Cut a few more small stars from the orange icing and stick these onto the big star as well.

Happy birthday!

YOU WILL NEED

» Large, round biscuit
» Plastic icing: different colours
» Royal icing
» Rolling pin

Method

1. Choose one colour icing as the background and roll it out.
2. Use the other colours to shape little snakes which are placed on the background.
3. Roll over the snakes lightly to flatten them and cut a shape the size of the biscuit.
4. Stick the design onto the biscuit with royal icing.
5. Use a piping bag and write the message on the biscuit.

Sixty!

This biscuit can be used when someone turns 60 or is celebrating a 60th anniversary.

YOU WILL NEED

» Flower-shaped biscuit
» Plastic icing: light purple, dark purple and white
» Flower-shaped cookie cutters: 1 large and 1 medium
» Number cookie cutters: 6 and 0
» Rolling pin

Method

1. Roll out the plastic icing; cut a large flower from the light purple icing. Stick it onto the flower-shaped biscuit using royal icing.
2. Cut smaller flowers from the dark purple and white icing. Make the white flower only slightly smaller than the dark purple one.
3. Cut the 6 and 0 from the dark purple icing and stick everything onto the biscuit as indicated.
4. Use a piping bag to make small white dots around the dark purple flower.

Templates

Shell fold – page 31 (enlarge by 123%)

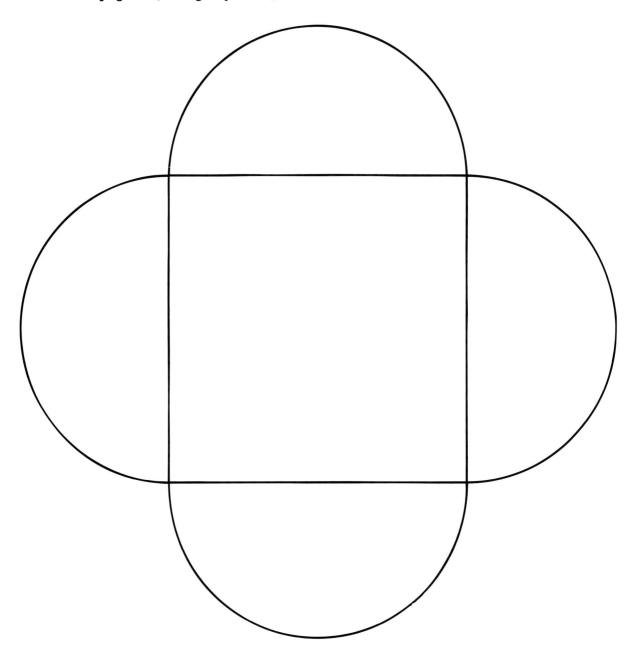

Dog and trailer filled with love – page 58

Simply white – page 61

Simply white – page 61

Reliable pewter – page 75

Ethnic copper – page 76

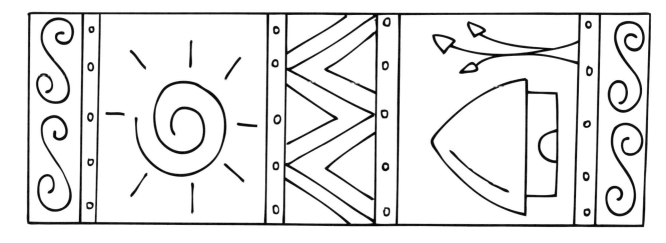

Iris oval – page 97

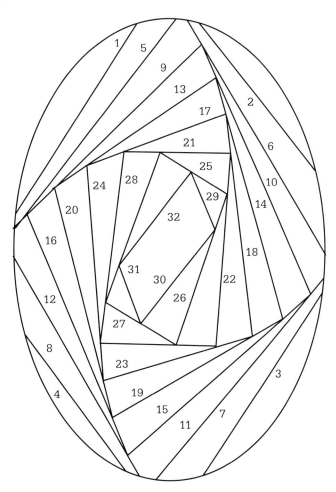

Come dance with me – page 98

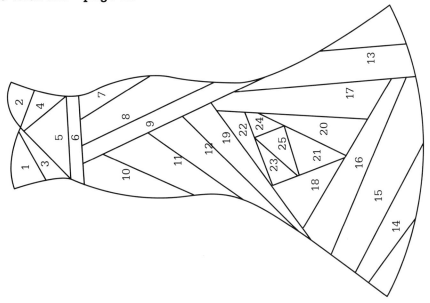

Brightly coloured flower card – page 99

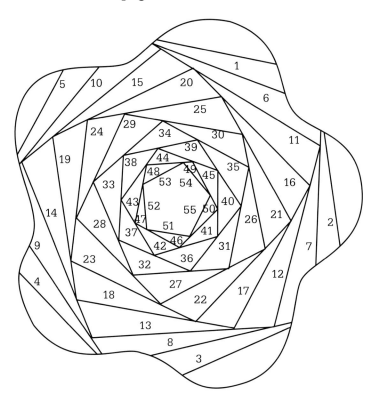

Iris heart – page 101

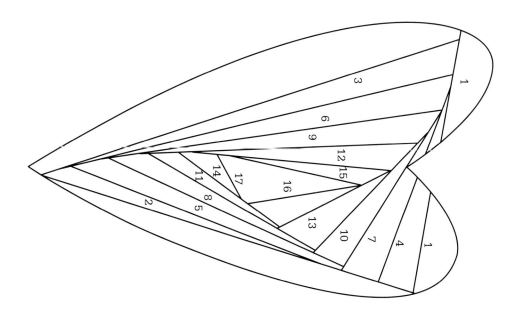

Christmas balls – page 100

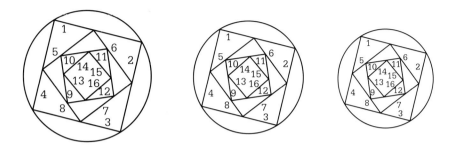

Yellow hat with rosette – page 111 (enlarge by 132%)

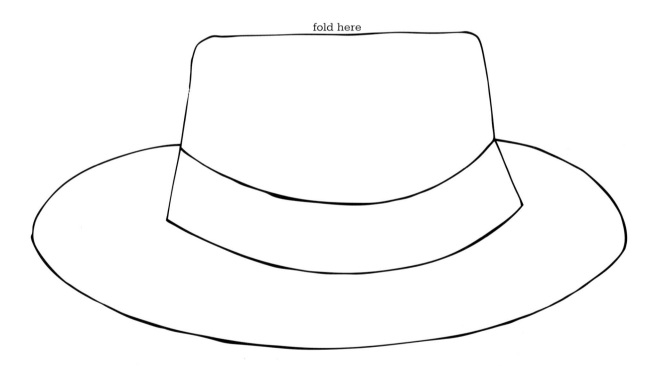

fold here

Red-and-green prick and stitch card – page 119

1. Make holes in the card on every dot using a pin.

2. The needle is inserted at A (from front to back) and is pulled out at each of the numbers (from back to front).

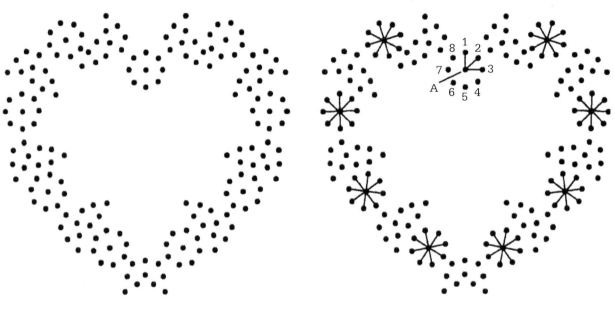

3.

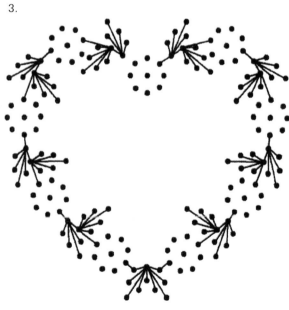

4.

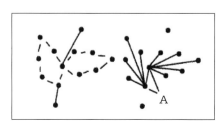

Sparkling spirelli – page 121

Japanese spirelli card – page 120

Multi-coloured African face – page 131

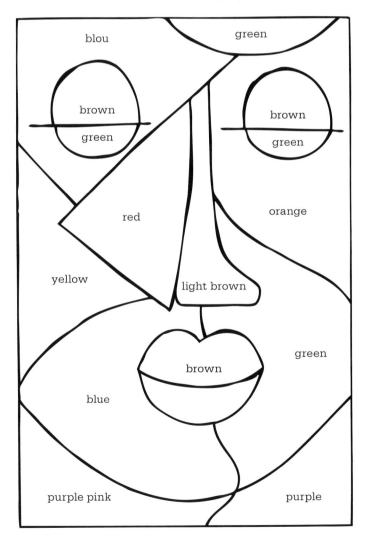

blou

green

brown

green

brown

green

red

orange

yellow

light brown

green

brown

blue

purple pink

purple

Cheerful butterfly – page 135

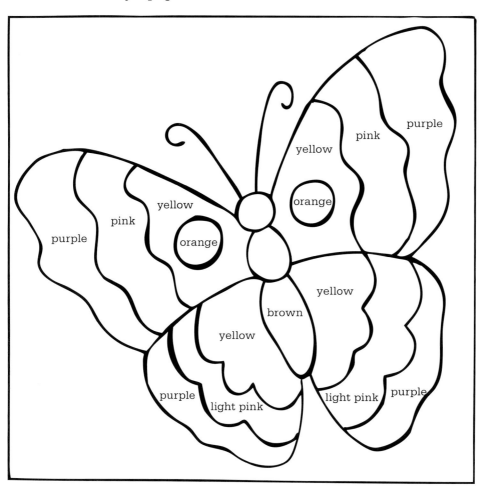

Cute cupcakes – page 153

small

large

large

small

cut here
for white

cut here
for white

In full bloom – page 154

Felt butterfly – page 155

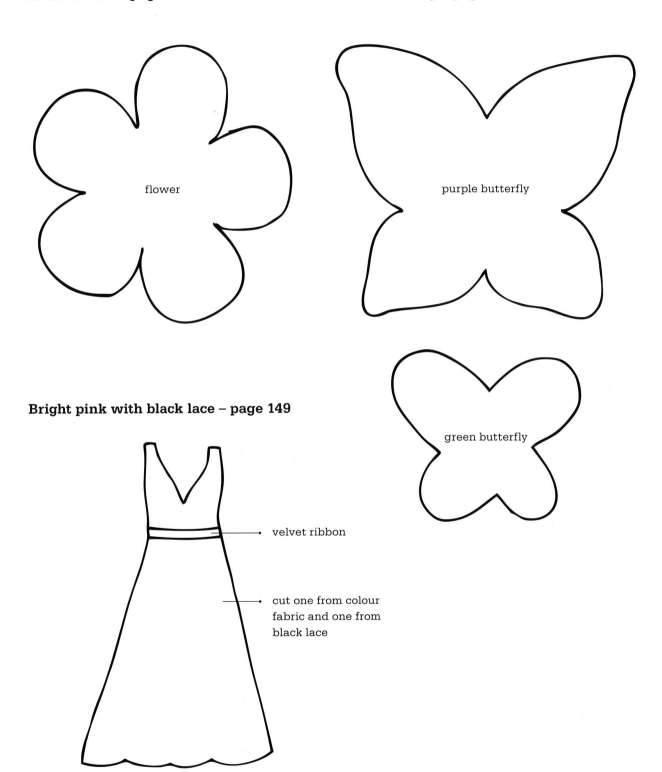

flower

purple butterfly

green butterfly

Bright pink with black lace – page 149

velvet ribbon

cut one from colour
fabric and one from
black lace

Classical cross – page 167

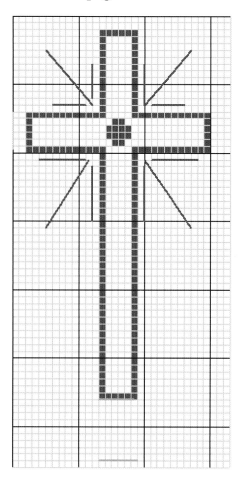

Grid size: 33 W x 66 H mm
Stitches: 30 x 63

DMC	Anchor	Description
*E301	-	metallic rust-brown
E168	301	metallic silver

Cute doggy – page 169

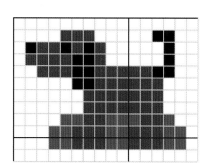

Grid size: 16 W x 12 H mm
Stitches: 14 x 10

DMC	Anchor	Description
310	403	black
433	371	brown - medium
700	229	Christmas green - bright
820	134	royal blue - very dark

For Christmas – page 168

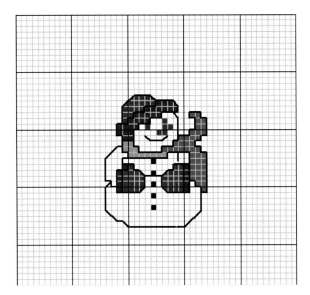

Grid size: 30 W x 28 H mm
Stitches: 27 x 25

DMC	Anchor	Description
666	46	Christmas red - bright
White	2	white
312	147	navy blue - light
*310	403	black
912	205	emerald green - light
910	228	emerald green - dark
498	20	Christmas red - dark

Metallic thread: E699, E703 (green),
E321 (red), E5200 (white)

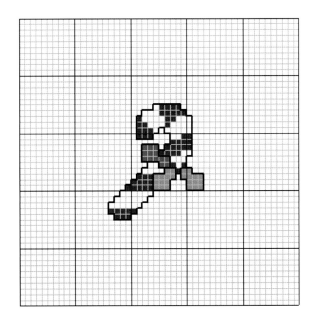

Grid size: 25 W x 25 H mm
Stitches: 22 x 22

DMC	Anchor	Description
White	2	white
*310	403	black
912	205	emerald green - light
304	47	Christmas red - medium
910	228	emerald green - dark

Metallic thread: E699, E703 (green),
E321 (red), E5200 (white)

Fransie Snyman

Science teacher **Fransie Snyman** has a
B. Ed. degree and a B. Sc. degree in Home
Economics. She has always been interested in
crafts and needlework despite her involvement
in the sciences. Although jewellery-making is
her first love, she loves paper and has always
made her own greetings cards. Dabbling
in many other crafts, including pewter,
scrapbooking, glass painting and encaustic
art, she belongs to several craft groups
and is a regular teacher at expos and other
gatherings. This is her seventh book.